TEACHER'S PET PUBLICATIONS

LITPLAN TEACHER PACK
for
One Day in the Life of Ivan Denisovich
based on the book by
Alexander Solzhenitsyn

Written by
Mary B. Collins

© 1996 Teacher's Pet Publications
All Rights Reserved

This **LitPlan** for Alexander Solzhenitsyn's
One Day in the Life of Ivan Denisovich
has been brought to you by Teacher's Pet Publications, Inc.

Copyright Teacher's Pet Publications 1996
11504 Hammock Point
Berlin MD 21811

Only the student materials in this unit plan (such as worksheets, study questions, and tests) may be reproduced multiple times for use in the purchaser's classroom.

For any additional copyright questions,
contact Teacher's Pet Publications.

www.tpet.com

TABLE OF CONTENTS - *One Day In The Life of Ivan Denisovich*

Introduction	6
Unit Objectives	7
Reading Assignment Sheet	8
Unit Outline	9
Study Questions (Short Answer)	13
Quiz/Study Questions (Multiple Choice)	20
Pre-reading Vocabulary Worksheets	31
Lesson One (Introductory Lesson)	41
Nonfiction Assignment Sheet	45
Oral Reading Evaluation Form	47
Writing Assignment 1	42
Writing Assignment 2	49
Writing Assignment 3	60
Writing Evaluation Form	52
Vocabulary Review Activities	56
Extra Writing Assignments/Discussion ?s	54
Unit Review Activities	62
Unit Tests	65
Unit Resource Materials	99
Vocabulary Resource Materials	115

A FEW NOTES ABOUT THE AUTHOR
Alexander Solzhenitsyn

SOLZHENITSYN, Alexander (born 1918). The favorite subject of exiled Soviet novelist and historian Alexander Solzhenitsyn is his homeland. Solzhenitsyn has chronicled the story of a world unto itself, the Soviet prison system.

Alexander Isayevich Solzhenitsyn was born on Dec. 11, 1918, in Kislovodsk, Russia. After graduating with a degree in mathematics from the University of Rostov-on-Don, Solzhenitsyn served in the Red Army artillery in World War II. In 1945 he was arrested for criticizing Joseph Stalin in a letter and was imprisoned for eight years. While imprisoned, Solzhenitsyn worked in a labor camp and a prison research institute and first began to write poetry. In prison he was also diagnosed as having cancer. After his release on the day of Stalin's death, Solzhenitsyn was forced to spend three years in exile.

His first book, 'One Day in the Life of Ivan Denisovich', published in Russian in 1962, tells the story of a day in the life of an inmate in a Soviet labor camp. The book brought Solzhenitsyn instant recognition. 'The First Circle' and 'Cancer Ward', both published abroad in 1968, made Solzhenitsyn an internationally famous figure.

Solzhenitsyn's criticism of government repression led to a ban on publication of his work in the Soviet Union after the mid-1960s. His books continued to be published abroad, however, and were circulated underground inside the Soviet Union. Solzhenitsyn was awarded the Nobel prize for literature in 1970 but was afraid to leave the Soviet Union to receive it for fear that the government would not allow him to reenter the country when he returned.

In 1974, shortly after the first parts of 'The Gulag Archipelago' were published in Paris, Solzhenitsyn was arrested and tried for treason. Exiled from the Soviet Union, he settled in Switzerland and finally took possession of his Nobel prize. He later settled in the United States. In 1980 he published 'The Mortal Danger' in English. Because of changes in official Soviet policy, most of his works once again became available to Soviet readers in 1989. In December 1989 Solzhenitsyn refused a Soviet offer to reinstate his citizenship.

--- Courtesy of Compton's Learning Center

INTRODUCTION

This unit has been designed to develop students' reading, writing, thinking, and language skills through exercises and activities related to *One Day In The Life of Ivan Denisovich* by Alexander Solzhenitsyn. It includes nineteen lessons, supported by extra resource materials.

The **introductory lesson** introduces students to some background to the novel through a **research assignment**. Following the introductory activity, students are given a transition to explain how the activity relates to the book they are about to read. Following the transition, students are given the materials they will be using during the unit. At the end of the lesson, students begin the pre-reading work for the first reading assignment.

The **reading assignments** are approximately thirty pages each; some are a little shorter while others are a little longer. Students have approximately 15 minutes of pre-reading work to do prior to each reading assignment. This pre-reading work involves reviewing the study questions for the assignment and doing some vocabulary work for 8 to 10 vocabulary words they will encounter in their reading.

The **study guide questions** are fact-based questions; students can find the answers to these questions right in the text. These questions come in two formats: short answer or multiple choice. The best use of these materials is probably to use the short answer version of the questions as study guides for students (since answers will be more complete), and to use the multiple choice version for occasional quizzes. If your school has the appropriate machinery, it might be a good idea to make transparencies of your answer keys for the overhead projector.

The **vocabulary work** is intended to enrich students' vocabularies as well as to aid in the students' understanding of the book. Prior to each reading assignment, students will complete a two-part worksheet for approximately 8 to 10 vocabulary words in the upcoming reading assignment. Part I focuses on students' use of general knowledge and contextual clues by giving the sentence in which the word appears in the text. Students are then to write down what they think the words mean based on the words' usage. Part II nails down the definitions of the words by giving students dictionary definitions of the words and having students match the words to the correct definitions based on the words' contextual usage. Students should then have an understanding of the words when they meet them in the text.

After each reading assignment, students will go back and formulate answers for the study guide questions. Discussion of these questions serves as a **review** of the most important events and ideas presented in the reading assignments.

After students complete reading the work, there is a **vocabulary review** lesson which pulls together all of the fragmented vocabulary lists for the reading assignments and gives students a review of all of the words they have studied.

A lesson is devoted to the **extra discussion questions/writing assignments**. These questions focus on interpretation, critical analysis and personal response, employing a variety of thinking skills and adding to the students' understanding of the novel.

There is one **group activity** in which students work in small groups to discuss themes in the novel.

The group activity is followed by a **reports and discussion** session in which the groups share their ideas about the themes with the entire class; thus, the entire class is exposed to information about all of the themes and the entire class can discuss each theme based on the nucleus of information brought forth by each of the groups.

There are three **writing assignments** in this unit, each with the purpose of informing, persuading, or having students express personal opinions. The first assignment is to inform: write a composition about the research they've done in preparation for an oral presentation. The second assignment is express personal opinions: students write a composition entitled *One Day in the Life of_____* (student's name). The third assignment is to persuade: students write a composition persuading someone to change something they don't like or think is unfair.

In addition, there is a **nonfiction reading assignment**. Students are required to read a piece of nonfiction related in some way to *One Day In The Life of Ivan Denisovich*. After reading their nonfiction pieces, students will fill out a worksheet on which they answer questions regarding facts, interpretation, criticism, and personal opinions.

The **review lesson** pulls together all of the aspects of the unit. The teacher is given four or five choices of activities or games to use which all serve the same basic function of reviewing all of the information presented in the unit.

The **unit test** comes in two formats: multiple choice or short answer. As a convenience, two different tests for each format have been included. There is also an advanced short answer test for students who need more of a challenge.

There are additional **support materials** included with this unit. The **extra activities section** includes suggestions for an in-class library, crossword and word search puzzles related to the novel, and extra vocabulary worksheets. There is a list of **bulletin board ideas** which gives the teacher suggestions for bulletin boards to go along with this unit. In addition, there is a list of **extra class activities** the teacher could choose from to enhance the unit or as a substitution for an exercise the teacher might feel is inappropriate for his/her class. **Answer keys** are located directly after the **reproducible student materials** throughout the unit. The student materials may be reproduced for use in the teacher's classroom without infringement of copyrights. No other portion of this unit may be reproduced without the written consent of Teacher's Pet Publications, Inc.

UNIT OBJECTIVES - *One Day In The Life of Ivan Denisovich*

1. To expose students to a different way of life; to show students that all countries are not democracies where people have recourse against injustice.

2. Students will demonstrate their understanding of the text on four levels: factual, interpretive, critical and personal.

3. Students will examine our criminal justice system and compare it to the one in *Ivan Denisovich*.

4. Students will be given the opportunity to practice reading aloud and silently to improve their skills in each area.

5. Students will answer questions to demonstrate their knowledge and understanding of the main events and characters in *One Day In The Life of Ivan Denisovich* as they relate to the author's theme development.

6. Students will enrich their vocabularies and improve their understanding of the novel through the vocabulary lessons prepared for use in conjunction with the novel.

7. The writing assignments in this unit are geared to several purposes:
    a. To have students demonstrate their abilities to inform, to persuade, or to express their own personal ideas
        Note: Students will demonstrate ability to write effectively to <u>inform</u> by developing and organizing facts to convey information. Students will demonstrate the ability to write effectively to <u>persuade</u> by selecting and organizing relevant information, establishing an argumentative purpose, and by designing an appropriate strategy for an identified audience. Students will demonstrate the ability to write effectively to <u>express personal ideas</u> by selecting a form and its appropriate elements.
    b. To check the students' reading comprehension
    c. To make students think about the ideas presented by the novel
    d. To encourage logical thinking
    e. To provide an opportunity to practice good grammar and improve students' use of the English language.

8. Students will read aloud, report, and participate in large and small group discussions to improve their public speaking and personal interaction skills.

READING ASSIGNMENT SHEET - *One Day in the Life of Ivan Denisovich*

Date Assigned	#	Assignment	Completion Date
	1	Beginning of book to ". . . his cheeks were falling in. But he had guts."	
	2	"Out beyond the camp boundary the intense cold..." to "All you got if you opened your mouth was a bunch of swearwords."	
	3	"The steppe was barren and windswept..." to "Once more they bushed everybody back from the gates...Form fives, First. Second...."	
	4	"What made this recounting so infuriating..." to "...they had nothing to do except unhook the door, let people through, and slip the hook on again."	
	5	"Shukhov came out with a full belly." to end of book	

UNIT OUTLINE - *One Day In The Life of Ivan Denisovich*

1 Research Assignment	2 Writing Assignment #1	3 Reports	4 PVR RA#1	5 Study ?s RA#1 PVR RA#2
6 Study ?s RA#2 Writing Assignment #2 PVR RA#3	7 Study ?s RA#3 PVR RA#4	8 Study ?s RA#4 PVR RA#5	9 Study ?s RA#5 Extra ?s	10 Discussion
11 Vocabulary	12 Group Activity	13 Reports & Discussion	14 Writing Assignment #3	15 Speaker
16 Reading Nonfiction	17 Discussion: Criminal Justice System	18 Review	19 Test	

Key: P=Preview Study Questions V=Prereading Vocabulary Worksheets R=Read RA=Reading Assignment

STUDY GUIDE QUESTIONS

SHORT ANSWER STUDY GUIDE QUESTIONS - *One Day In The Life of Ivan Denisovich*

Reading Assignment #1
1. Who is Ivan Denisovich Shukhov?
2. Why didn't Shukhov rise at reveille?
3. Who are Tyurin and Pavlo?
4. The Tartar sentenced Ivan Denisovich to three days penalty with work for oversleeping. How did Ivan get out of serving that sentence?
5. Ivan did a lousy job of washing the guardroom floor. Why?
6. Identify Alyosha the Baptist, Buinovsky and Fetiukov.
7. Why was it better to hide around a corner than to be seen by a guard alone?
8. What happened when Ivan went to the doctor?
9. Why did Ivan hide his bread?
10. How did the 104th get out of being sent to the "Socialist Way of Life Settlement" to work?
11. Why did Tsezar Markovich give Ivan his cigarette butt instead of giving it to Fetiukov?
12. Who was Lieutenant Volkovoi?
13. What was the result of the "undershirt search"?

Reading Assignment #2
14. "The thoughts of a prisoner -- they're not free either." Why not?
15. Why didn't Ivan write to his family more often?
16. Why didn't Ivan want to be a carpet painter after his release?
17. "That wasn't the way to eat, he learned in camp. You had to eat with all of your mind on the food ---." Why did Ivan think that?
18. Why were snowstorms both a blessing and a curse to the prisoners?
19. The experienced prisoners get by by stashing useful things and economizing. Give at least four examples.
20. Why did Ivan like to work?
21. What kind of work did Fetiukov and the captain have? Why was that ironic?
22. Why did Ivan tell Kilgas he shouldn't worry about his 25 years?
23. What were the circumstances leading to Ivan's incarceration?
24. Why did the men often have short rations?

Ivan Denisovich Short Answer Study Questions Page 2

Reading Assignment #3
25. How did Ivan manage to get extra bowls of food for his squad?
26. The idea that the squad works together for mutual benefit or honor is shown several times. Give at least two examples.
27. Who was Der?
28. Why did Ivan keep working after it was time to quit?
29. Where do the people of Ivan's village say the old moon goes?

Reading Assignment #4
30. Who was missing at the count, and what happened to him when he was found?
31. How did the 104th exert it's independence on the way back from work?
32. What favor did Ivan volunteer to do for Tsezar? Why?
33. Why didn't Ivan get caught with the piece of hacksaw blade when he was searched?
34. Why didn't Ivan get parcels of his own?
35. What was Ivan's reward for holding a place in line for Tsezar?
36. Identify the Limper.

Reading Assignment #5

37. Where did Ivan go after dinner?
38. Why was Alyosha glad to be in prison?
39. What was Ivan's view of religion?
40. What strokes of luck had Ivan had that day?

ANSWER KEY: SHORT ANSWER STUDY GUIDE QUESTIONS
One Day In The Life of Ivan Denisovich

<u>Reading Assignment #1</u>

1. Who is Ivan Denisovich Shukhov?

    He is a prisoner at a "special" labor camp in Russia. "S854"

2. Why didn't Shukhov rise at reveille?

    He wasn't feeling well that morning. He decided to take a chance on getting caught, and wait until the last minute to get up.

3. Who are Tyurin and Pavlo?

    Tyurin is Ivan's squad leader; Pavlo is Tyurin's deputy. They get the work assignments and keep the men in order.

4. The Tartar sentenced Ivan Denisovich to three days penalty with work for oversleeping. How did Ivan get out of serving that sentence?

    The Tartar really only wanted someone to clean the guardroom floor, so he let the sentence go.

5. Ivan did a lousy job of washing the guardroom floor. Why?

    "When you worked for the knowing you gave them quality; when you worked for a fool you simply gave him eyewash."

6. Identify Alyosha the Baptist, Buinovsky and Fetiukov.

    They were members of Ivan's squad. Alyosha is Ivan's "top tier neighbor" at the barracks. Buinovsky, an ex-naval captain, bunked below Alyosha. Fetiukov was lower in "rank" than Ivan in the squad.

7. Why was it better to hide around a corner than to be seen by a guard alone?

    The guards were often looking for an excuse to penalize prisoners. The hat regulation and other regulations equally as ridiculous made it easy for guards to do what they wanted to do with prisoners.

8. What happened when Ivan went to the doctor?

    He was refused sick leave. His temperature was under 100 and two others had already been excused, so he had to go to work.

9. Why did Ivan hide his bread?

    He wanted to save it for later so it wouldn't be stolen.

10. How did the 104th get out of being sent to the "Socialist Way of Life Settlement" to work?
    The squad leader, Tyurin, had bribed the officials at the planning department with salt pork.

11. Why did Tsezar Markovich give Ivan his cigarette butt instead of giving it to Fetiukov?
    Fetiukov had interrupted his chain of thought by begging for the butt. Ivan had been patient and silent and had not lowered himself to verbally begging Tsezar.

12. Who was Lieutenant Volkovoi?
    He was the security chief. "Volk" means "wolf." He was mean and harsh with the prisoners.

13. What was the result of the "undershirt search"?
    Ivan was in regulation dress. Tsezar had a flannel vest. Buinovsky had a vest and protested and got ten days in the guardhouse.

Reading Assignment #2
14. "The thoughts of a prisoner -- they're not free either." Why not?
    "They kept returning to the same things." (food, warmth, fate of self and fellow prisoners)

15. Why didn't Ivan write to his family more often?
    He didn't have anything in common with them anymore; he had more in common with the other prisoners. He had no news and little hope.

16. Why didn't Ivan want to be a carpet painter after his release?
    He didn't think it was an honest profession like carpentry or plumbing. "Easy money weighs light in the hand and doesn't give you the feeling you've earned it."

17. "That wasn't the way to eat, he learned in camp. You had to eat with all of your mind on the food--." Why did Ivan think that?
    He considered the large amount of work he had done while in the camp eating a small amount of food (rather than always being full).

18. Why were snowstorms both a blessing and a curse to the prisoners?
    The prisoners got off of work for snow days but had to make them up by working Sundays.

19. The experienced prisoners get by by stashing useful things and economizing. Give at least four examples.
    bread -- trowel -- roll of roofing felt -- hacksaw blade

20. Why did Ivan like to work?

    It made time go fast, made him forget his troubles and worries, and it gave him something he could be proud of.

21. What kind of work did Fetiukov and the captain have? Why was that ironic?

    They were both in positions of responsibility in the outside world, but in camp they were doing labor, bringing up loads of sand. Ivan was just an average man but was given responsible jobs as one of the best workers at the camp. Their roles were reversed.

22. Why did Ivan tell Kilgas he shouldn't worry about his 25 years?

    "It's not a fact you'll be in all that time. But I've been in eight full years -- now that's a fact." In other words, only the past is a fact. The future is uncertain at best. Live for now, do the best you can, and the future will take care of itself.

23. What were the circumstances leading to Ivan's incarceration?

    He was sentenced for high treason. He had agreed to carry out a mission for German intelligence. He had a choice of carrying out the mission or being killed, so he agreed to carry out the mission.

24. Why did the men often have short rations?

    The cook paid his helpers with extra portions of food. Since the cook was lazy, he had a lot of people to pay, and the men often had short portions.

Reading Assignment #3

25. How did Ivan manage to get extra bowls of food for his squad?

    He and Pavlo mixed up the cook's count and managed to get extra.

26. The idea that the squad works together for mutual benefit or honor is shown several times. Give at least two examples.

    -- All going to work early after lunch
    -- All running in for the evening (to beat the other squad)
    -- Mortar men keeping up with masons

27. Who was Der?

    He was the building foreman who complained about the men's work and the roofing felt over the windows. He backed down when the men physically threatened him.

28. Why did Ivan keep working after it was time to quit?

    There was mortar left, which would freeze and be useless if it wasn't used up. He worried about anything he could make use of, about every scrap of work he could do. Nothing must be wasted without good reason.

29. Where do the people of Ivan's village say the old moon goes?
    God crumbles it up and makes stars.

Reading Assignment #4

30. Who was missing at the count, and what happened to him when he was found?
    The Moldavian was missing. When he came back, everyone called him names, the guard hit him, and a Hungarian kicked him.

31. How did the 104th exert it's independence on the way back from work?
    They ignored the guards who were telling them to hurry up. Yet, when they decided to "race" the column from the machineworks, they all ran without the guards' command to do so.

32. What favor did Ivan volunteer to do for Tsezar? Why?
    He offered to stand in line at the parcels office. He hoped to get a part of the parcel as a payment -- or to sell the place in line if there was no parcel.

33. Why didn't Ivan get caught with the piece of hacksaw blade when he was searched?
    It was just luck. He hid it in his mitten. Because the chief was in a hurry, he didn't bother checking the mitten.

34. Why didn't Ivan get parcels of his own?
    He told his family not to send them. "Don't take food out of the kids' mouths."

35. What was Ivan's reward for holding a place in line for Tsezar?
    Tsezar gave him his dinner portion and bread.

36. Identify the Limper.
    He was the mess hall orderly who admitted the prisoners for meals. He was ill-tempered and frequently used his club on the prisoners.

Reading Assignment #5

37. Where did Ivan go after dinner?
    He went to the Lett's room to buy tobacco.

38. Why was Alyosha glad to be in prison?
    "Here you have time to think about your soul."

39. What was Ivan's view of religion?
    "I'm not against God, understand that. I do believe in God. But I don't believe in paradise or in hell. . . . somehow it works out all right for you [Alyosha]: Jesus Christ wanted you to sit in prison and so you are -- sitting there for His sake. But for whose sake am I here?"

40. What strokes of luck had Ivan had that day?

"He'd had many strokes of luck that day: they hadn't put him in the cells; they hadn't sent his squad to the settlement; he'd swiped a bowl of kasha at dinner; the squad leader had fixed the rates well; he'd built a wall and enjoyed doing it; he's smuggled that bit of hacksaw blade through; he'd earned a favor from Tsezar that evening; he'd bought that tobacco. And he hadn't fallen ill."

MULTIPLE CHOICE STUDY GUIDE/QUIZ QUESTIONS
One Day In The Life of Ivan Denisovich

Reading Assignment #1

1. Who is Ivan Denisovich Shukhov?
    a. He is the head guard at a "special" labor camp in Russia.
    b. He is a writer who met a former prisoner from a labor camp. He is telling the prisoner's story.
    c. He is a prisoner at a "special" labor camp in Russia.
    d. He is the son of a former prisoner, now reading his father's memoirs.

2. Why didn't Shukhov rise at reveille?
    a. He wasn't feeling well. He decided to take a chance on getting caught, and wait until the last minute to get up.
    b. He was trying to get the guard angry. It was the way he amused himself.
    c. He's hearing was failing, and the authorities would not do anything to help him. He simply didn't hear the reveille call.
    d. He was hoping to get put in the stockade, thus avoiding work for a few days.

3. Who are Tyurin and Pavlo?
    a. They are fellow prisoners. They are forming an escape plan.
    b. They are doctors who enjoy experimenting on the prisoners.
    c. They are two vicious guard dogs who follow the prisoners around all day. They attack anyone who goes too close to the gates.
    d. They are the squad leader and deputy. They get the work assignments and keep the men in order.

4. The Tartar sentenced Ivan to three days penalty with work for oversleeping. How did Ivan get out of serving that sentence?
    a. He gave the Tartar half of his food rations for a week.
    b. He cleaned the guardroom floor.
    c. He wrote a letter to the Tartar's family for him, since the Tartar couldn't write.
    d. He informed on one of this squad mates, making the Tartar look good.

5. True or False: Ivan did a lousy job washing the guardroom floor.
    a. True
    b. False

6. True or False: Alyosha, Buinovsky, and Fetiukov are prisoners in another squad. They are vicious and attack the men in Ivan's squad at the slightest provocation.
    a. True
    b. False

Ivan Multiple Choice Study Questions Page 2

7. Which was better for the prisoners; to hide around a corner or to be seen by a guard alone?
    a. It was better to hide around a corner.
    b. It was better to be seen alone.

8. What happened when Ivan went to the doctor?
    a. He got two days in the infirmary.
    b. He got an extra work duty for complaining.
    c. The doctor gave him a shot and told him to lie down for an hour, and then be rechecked.
    d. He was refused sick leave. His temperature was under 100.

9. What did Ivan do with his bread?
    a. He ate it quickly because he was so hungry.
    b. He used it to bribe a guard into giving him a lighter work detail.
    c. He saved it in his mattress so it would not be stolen.
    d. He gave it to a fellow prisoner who was very ill.

10. How did the 104th get out of being sent to the "Socialist Way of Life Settlement" to work?
    a. They won a coin toss determining who would not have to go.
    b. They traded two pairs of valenkis for the privilege of staying behind.
    c. They squad leader had bribed the officials at the planning department with salt pork.
    d. They simply refused to go. They decided they would rather take a punishment. In frustration, the guards sent another squad.

11. What did Tsezer Markovich do with his cigarette butt?
    a. He ground it under his heel in front of the prisoners, just to show his power.
    b. He gave it to Ivan, who had been waiting patiently.
    c. He put it in his pocket, intending to use it later as a bribe.
    d. He sold it to Fetiukov.

12. True or False; Lieutenant Volkovoy was the security chief. He was mean and harsh with the prisoners. His name mean "wolf."
    a. True
    b. False

13. Which of the following was not a result of the "undershirt search?"
    a. Ivan was in regulation dress.
    b. Tsezar had a flannel vest.
    c. Tiurin had no undershirt.
    d. Buinovsky had a vest.

Ivan Multiple Choice Study Questions Page 3

Reading Assignment #2

14. True or False: The author states that: "At least the thoughts of the prisoners are free."
    a. True
    b. False

15. Why didn't Ivan write to his family more often?
    a. He was not allowed to write more than one letter a year.
    b. He didn't know how to write, and he didn't want to use his bread ration to pay someone to do it for him.
    c. He didn't have enough money to pay for the paper, envelope and postage.
    d. He didn't have anything in common with them. He had little news, and little hope.

16. Why didn't Ivan want to be a carpet painter after his release?
    a. He didn't think it was an honest profession.
    b. He was allergic to many of the chemicals used in the process.
    c. He had been told he didn't possess the necessary skills.
    d. Carpet painters didn't make much money. He wanted a lucrative job.

17. Which of the following statements tells what Ivan thought about food?
    a. Since the food was so bad and scarce, it was best to think of other things while eating.
    b. You should eat with all of your mind on the food.

18. Why were snowstorms both a blessing and a curse to the prisoners?
    a. They were beautiful to look at, but treacherous to work in.
    b. It was easier to escape in a snowstorm, but because of this, the men were shackled at the ankle whenever they went somewhere.
    c. The prisoners got off work for snow days but had to make it up on Sundays.
    d. They guards were usually a bit lax, because they couldn't do much outside work, but the prisoners got bored and started fighting when they didn't have enough to do.

19. They experienced prisoners get by by stashing useful things and economizing. Which of the following is not one of the items they hoard?
    a. Spoons
    b. Bread
    c. Trowel
    d. Hacksaw blade

Ivan Multiple Choice Study Questions Page 4

20. How did Ivan feel about work?
    a. He liked it. It made time go fast and he forgot his troubles and worries. It gave him something to be proud of.
    b. He hated it. He resented working without pay.

21. Fetiukov and the captain had positions of responsibility in the outside world, but in camp they were doing labor. Ivan was just an average man but was given responsible jobs as one of the best workers in the camp. What is this literary devise called?
    a. Reversibility
    b. Irony
    c. Metamorphosis
    d. Sarcasm

22. What did Ivan tell Kilgas about his 25 year sentence?
    a. Live for now, do the best you can, and the future will take care of itself.
    b. Plan for the future. It will take your mind off of the daily drudgery.

23. What were the circumstances leading to Ivan's incarceration?
    a. He had murdered a member of the police force during a riot.
    b. He was trying to defect to the United States. Someone informed on him, and he was imprisoned.
    c. He was accused of writing and distributing subversive literature to members of the army and to the general populace.
    d. He was a member of the Soviet army. His squad had been captured by the Germans, but he and a few others had escaped. When they made it back to their own lives, their story was not believed. They were accused of collaborating with the Germans.

24. Why did the men often have short rations?
    a. The officials frequently starved the prisoners out of their own sadistic impulses.
    b. Gas was in short supply and the food delivery trucks could not always deliver on schedule.
    c. There simply wasn't enough food in the country, and the politicians and military personnel were fed first.
    d. The cook paid his many helpers with extra portions of food.

Ivan Multiple Choice Study Questions Page 5

<u>Reading Assignment #3</u>

25. How did Ivan manage to get extra bowls of food for his squad?
    a. He bribed the cook.
    b. He mixed up the bowl count and confused the cook.
    c. The cook liked Ivan because he was always polite and helpful. He gave Ivan the extra food.
    d. He stole them when the cook was busy.

26. The idea that the squad worked together for mutual benefit or honor is shown several times. Which of these is <u>not</u> an example?
    a. Sharing food packages.
    b. All going to work early after lunch.
    c. All running in for the evening to beat the other squad.
    d. Mortar men keeping up with Masons.

27. Who was Der?
    a. He was the Commandant's secretary. He snuggled mail in and out for the prisoners.
    b. He was the building foreman who complained about the men's work and the roofing felt over the windows. He backed down when the men physically threatened him.
    c. He was a new prisoner who had just come to the squad. The others thought he was an informant.
    d. He was the commander of the camp. He was very punitive and enjoyed tormenting the prisoners.

28. Why did Ivan keep working after it was time to quit?
    a. He was trying to earn extra bread.
    b. He had asked for a few hours off for the following day. The squad leader agreed, but he had to make the time up ahead of time.
    c. There was mortar left, and he wanted to use it up before it froze.
    d. He was obsessed with working, because it kept his mind off his loneliness.

29. Where do the people of Ivan's village say the old moon goes?
    a. It gets eaten by the North Wind.
    b. It goes to America.
    c. It falls off the horizon and gets melted by the sun.
    d. God crumbles it up and makes stars.

Ivan Multiple Choice Study Questions Page 6

<u>Reading Assignment #4</u>

30. Who was missing at the count, and what happened to him when he was found?
    a. The Moldavian was missing. When he came back, everyone called him names, the guard hit him, and a Hungarian kicked him.
    b. Fetiukov was missing. The others cheered when he came back. They were glad he had at least tried to escape.
    c. Kilgas was missing. When he returned, the others refused to have him in their bunk-house. They didn't want to be associated with him, for fear they would be punished.
    d. Senka was missing. Because the others liked him, they tried to protect him, but their attempts were not successful.

31. How did the 104th exert its independence on the way back from work?
    a. They marched with their hands in their pockets, even though they were supposed to have their hands behind their backs.
    b. They violated the silence rule by singing.
    c. They ignored the guards who were telling them to hurry up. Yet, when they decided to "race" the column from the machine works, they all ran without the guards' command.
    d. They lined up in rows of seven instead of their proper number. Then, while they were marching, they re-arranged themselves, sometimes having rows of 9, sometimes 4.

32. What favor did Ivan volunteer to do for Tsezar and why?
    a. He wrote a letter to Tsezar's wife because Tsezar couldn't write.
    b. He mended Tsezar's torn jacket. While doing this, he made a small, pocket on the inside where Tsezar could hide cigarettes and other items. Tsezar paid him 2 rubles.
    c. He did part of Tsezar's work for the day, hoping he could get an infirmary pass later.
    d. He offered to stand in line at the parcels office. He hoped to get a part of the parcel as payment, or to sell the place in line if there was no parcel.

33. Why didn't Ivan get caught with the piece of hacksaw blade when he was searched?
    a. He had cleverly and carefully hidden it in the hollow heel of his boot.
    b. It was just luck. The chief was in a hurry and didn't search him thoroughly.
    c. He had bribed the guard, who now overlooked the blade.
    d. He had such a reputation for trust-worthiness that the guard didn't put much effort into searching him. In his eight years in prison, he had never been caught with anything.

Ivan Multiple Choice Study Questions Page 7

34. Why didn't Ivan get parcel so his own?
   a. His family had disowned him when he was sent to prison.
   b. His family was too poor to send him anything.
   c. He had told his wife not to send them; he didn't want his children to be deprived.
   d. He had no close family who could send anything. His wife was in a women's prison, and his children were living with relatives and friends.

35. What was Ivan's reward for doing the favor for Tsezar?
   a. He got a pack of cigarettes.
   b. Tsezar gave him his dinner portion and bread.
   c. He got an extra pair of footrags.
   d. He got one day removed from his sentence.

36. Identify the Limper.
   a. He was the camp secretary who kept track of all of the mail and parcels. He received favor and bribes from almost everyone.
   b. He was a prisoner whose legs had been severely beaten by the guards when he was caught trying to escape. He was now used as a threat, to show the other prisoners what could happen to them.
   c. He was the orderly in the infirmary. He would slip pills to prisoners who paid him.
   d. He was the mess hall orderly who admitted prisoners for meals. He was ill-tempered and frequently used his club on the prisoners.

Ivan Multiple Choice Study Questions Page 8

<u>Reading Assignment #5</u>

37. Where did Ivan go after dinner?
    a. He went to the infirmary. He was hoping to be relieved of work for the next day.
    b. He went to his bunk and went to sleep.
    c. He went to the Lett's room to buy tobacco.
    d. He went to Pavlo's bunk. Pavlo had a deck of cards, and they were going to play poker.

38. Why was Alyosha glad to be in prison?
    a. He had no family and few friends. At least in prison he had company, food and a place to sleep.
    b. He had taken his son's place in prison. He was glad to make the sacrifice so his son could be free.
    c. He enjoyed having the time to think about his soul.
    d. He was mentally unstable. He truly believed that he had committed a crime against the state, and deserved to be punished.

39. What was Ivan's view of religion?
    a. He didn't believe in God at all. He said that if there were a God, there would be no wars or prisons.
    b. He was a devout man who believed wholeheartedly and prayed every day.
    c. He had, at one time, believed in God. Now he was not sure.
    d. He believed in God, but not in paradise or in hell.

40. When Ivan was falling asleep, he thought of the strokes of luck he had had that day. Which of the following was <u>not</u> one of his strokes of luck?
    a. He was first in line at mealtime.
    b. He had enjoyed building the wall.
    c. He had smuggled the bit of hacksaw blade through.
    d. He had been healthy.

ANSWER KEY - MULTIPLE CHOICE STUDY/QUIZ QUESTIONS
One Day In The Life of Ivan Denisovich

1.	C		21.	B
2.	A		22.	A
3.	D		23.	D
4.	B		24.	D
5.	A		25.	B
6.	B		26.	A
7.	A		27.	B
8.	D		28.	C
9.	C		29.	D
10.	C		30.	A
11.	B		31.	C
12.	A		32.	D
13.	A		33.	B
14.	B		34.	C
15.	D		35.	B
16.	A		36.	D
17.	B		37.	C
18.	C		38.	C
19.	A		39.	D
20.	A		40.	A

PREREADING VOCABULARY WORKSHEETS

Vocabulary - *One Day In The Life of Ivan Denisovich*

Reading Assignment 1
Part I: Using Prior Knowledge and Contextual Clues
    Below are the sentences in which the vocabulary words appear in the text. Read the sentence. Use any clues you can find in the sentence combined with your prior knowledge, and write what you think the underlined words mean on the lines provided.

1. The intermittent sounds barely penetrated the windowpanes

___

2. . . . announcing to no one in particular but with a sort of malicious glee: "Well, sailors, grit your teeth.. . ."

___

3. His crumpled, hairless face was imperturbable.

___

4. . . . he had known various systems for allocating footwear . . . .

___

5. Shukhov stamped his feet in vexation.

___

6. . . . Stepan Grigorych, the doctor who advocated work therapy.

___

7. Shukhov had finished his last pinch of tobacco and saw no prospects of acquiring any more before evening.

___

8. . . . the guards . . . now flung themselves into their work with savage zeal.

___

Ivan Vocabulary for Reading Assignment 1 Continued

Part II: Determining the Meaning

You have tried to figure out the meanings of the vocabulary words for Reading Assignment One. Now match the vocabulary words to their dictionary definitions. If there are words for which you cannot figure out the definition by contextual clues and by process of elimination, look them up in a dictionary.

___ 1. intermittent
___ 2. malicious
___ 3. imperturbable
___ 4. allocating
___ 5. vexation
___ 6. advocated
___ 7. acquiring
___ 8. zeal

A. unshakably calm and collected
B. supported the cause or idea of something
C. stopping and starting at intervals
D. gaining possession of
E. zest; energy
F. showing a desire to see others suffer
G. distributing according to a plan
H. annoyance

Vocabulary - *One Day In The Life of Ivan Denisovich* Reading Assignment Two

Part I: Using Prior Knowledge and Contextual Clues
   Below are the sentences in which the vocabulary words appear in the text. Read the sentence. Use any clues you can find in the sentence combined with your prior knowledge, and write what you think the underlined words mean on the lines provided.

9. To meet the contingency of a headwind he had got himself a cloth with a long tape at each end.

_____

10. Tiurin had only to lift an eyebrow or beckon with a finger--and you ran and did what he wanted.

_____

11. And although the 104th had been sitting there barely twenty minutes and the working day--curtailed because it was winter--didn't end till six, everyone felt already they'd had a rare stroke of luck . . . .

_____

12. But he'd already learned cunning: he ate the contents of his food packages alone, sometimes during the night.

_____

13. Shukhov didn't begrudge him his energy . . . .

_____

14. (good fat didn't reach the zeks, and the rancid all went into the soup kettle, so when there was an issue of rancid fat from the warehouse, the zeks welcomed it as an extra)

_____

Part II: Determining the Meaning
   You have tried to figure out the meanings of the vocabulary words for Reading Assignment Two. Now match the vocabulary words to their dictionary definitions. If there are words for which you cannot figure out the definition by contextual clues and by process of elimination, look them up in a dictionary.

___ 9. contingency   A. the art of subtlety and deceptiveness
___ 10. beckon   B. spoiled; gone bad
___ 11. curtailed   C. envy the possession or enjoyment of
___ 12. cunning   D. a possibility that must be prepared for
___ 13. begrudge   E. cut short
___ 14. rancid   F. to make a summoning gesture

Vocabulary - *One Day In The Life of Ivan Denisovich* Reading Assignment 3

Part I: Using Prior Knowledge and Contextual Clues
　　Below are the sentences in which the vocabulary words appear in the text. Read the sentence. Use any clues you can find in the sentence combined with your prior knowledge, and write what you think the underlined words mean on the lines provided.

15. This is a moment that demands complete concentration, as you remove some of the scanty kasha from the bottom of the bowl, put it carefully into your mouth, ...

_____

16. . . . they were transforming him from an eager, confident naval officer with a ringing voice into an inert, though wary, zek.

_____

17. And then, the vicious political idea--the justification of personal tyranny.

_____

18. A mockery of the memory of three generations of Russian intelligentsia.

_____

19. Where was all his arrogance?

_____

20. Tiurin looked at him witheringly. "Mind your own business, squirt. Bring some blocks."

_____

Part II: Determining the Meaning
　　You have tried to figure out the meanings of the vocabulary words for Chapter 5 & 6. Now match the vocabulary words to their dictionary definitions. If there are words for which you cannot figure out the definition by contextual clues and by process of elimination, look them up in a dictionary.

　　___ 15. scanty　　　　A. ridiculing; jeering at; making fun of
　　___ 16. inert　　　　　B. devastatingly
　　___ 17. vicious　　　　C. overbearing pride
　　___ 18. mockery　　　D. barely sufficient; a small amount
　　___ 19. arrogance　　 E. savage; faulty; foul
　　___ 20. witheringly　　F. unable to move or act

Vocabulary - *One Day In The Life of Ivan Denisovich* Reading Assignment 4

Part I: Using Prior Knowledge and Contextual Clues
    Below are the sentences in which the vocabulary words appear in the text. Read the sentence. Use any clues you can find in the sentence combined with your prior knowledge, and write what you think the underlined words mean on the lines provided.

21. Now he was chilled to the bone and his <u>fury</u> mounted with everyone else's; were they to be kept waiting another half hour by that Moldavian?
_____

22. This must be around the <u>consulting</u> hour.
_____

23. And now Shukhov was on the point of being frisked. Today he had nothing to <u>conceal</u>.
_____

24. Shukhov could try a <u>ruse</u>.
_____

25. They passed through the gates, those zeks, like soldiers back from a campaign, brisk, <u>taut</u>, eager-- clear the road for 'em.
_____

26. No splashes. He managed, too, to <u>maneuver</u> the tray so that the two bowls with the thickest stew were just opposite the place he was about to sit down in.
_____

Part II: Determining the Meaning
    You have tried to figure out the meanings of the vocabulary words for Reading Assignment 4. Now match the vocabulary words to their dictionary definitions. If there are words for which you cannot figure out the definition by contextual clues and by process of elimination, look them up in a dictionary.

___ 21. fury   A. hide
___ 22. consulting   B. tight; in shape; tense
___ 23. conceal   C. rage; anger
___ 24. ruse   D. a controlled change in movement, direction or position
___ 25. taut   E. seeking advise or information from someone
___ 26. maneuver   F. a crafty strategy; a diversion

Vocabulary - *One Day In The Life of Ivan Denisovich* Reading Assignment 5

Part I: Using Prior Knowledge and Contextual Clues
Below are the sentences in which the vocabulary words appear in the text. Read the sentence. Use any clues you can find in the sentence combined with your prior knowledge, and write what you think the underlined words mean on the lines provided.

27. Two hundred voices in Shukhov's half of the barracks were making a terrific din, but he fancied he heard the rail being struck.

_____

28. He was on the point of leaving when he felt a twinge of pity for Tsezar.

_____

29. He put his boots on the stove--first-comer's prerogative--then back to Tsezar's bunk.

_____

30. Impractical, that's his trouble. Makes himself nice to everyone but doesn't know how to do favors that get paid back.

_____

Part II: Determining the Meaning
You have tried to figure out the meanings of the vocabulary words for Chapters 7-10. Now match the vocabulary words to their dictionary definitions. If there are words for which you cannot figure out the definition by contextual clues and by process of elimination, look them up in a dictionary.

___ 27. din   A. exclusive right or privilege to choose
___ 28. twinge   B. not practical in nature; can't see or implement useful ideas
___ 29. prerogative   C. a jumble of loud, discordant sounds
___ 30. impractical   D. a sudden, sharp emotional or physical pain

ANSWER KEY - VOCABULARY
One Day In The Life of Ivan Denisovich

Reading Assignment One
1. C
2. F
3. A
4. G
5. H
6. B
7. D
8. E

Reading Assignment Two
9. D
10. F
11. E
12. A
13. C
14. B

Reading Assignment Three
15. D
16. F
17. E
18. A
19. C
20. B

Reading Assignment Four
21. C
22. E
23. A
24. F
25. B
26. D

Reading Assignment Five
27. C
28. D
29. A
30. B

DAILY LESSONS

LESSON ONE

Objectives
    1. To introduce the *Ivan Denisovich* unit
    2. To give students some background information about Russia
    3. To inform students about life in Russia
    4. To give students the opportunity to practice using the library's resources

Activity #1

    Take students to your school library where they will be able to find information about Russia.
    Explain to students that the class will be reading a book about a prisoner in a Soviet Russian work camp. Before reading the book, though, they are going to learn a little about Russia.
    Assign one of the following research topics to each of your students: history, music & art, tourist sights, work, medical care, religion, transportation , traditions, holidays, education, literature, media, geography, economy, food, government, current issues, shopping, worklife, sports, leisure activities, architecture, natural resources, and military. If you have more students than topics, add more topics or let students pair up on some of the bigger topics. History, for example could be divided into several chunks, as could government and other topics.
    Explain to students that they will be asked to give a short oral report about their topics, lasting 2-3 minutes. Today they should gather information and take notes. In the next class period they will be given time to organize their notes and put together their reports.
    Give students the remainder of this class time to do their research.

NOTE: Asking students to use a visual aide makes the oral presentations more interesting. The person talking about food could prepare a Russian dish, the tourist sights reporter could find slides or pictures to show, etc.

LESSON TWO

Objectives
    1. To give students the opportunity to practice writing to inform
    2. To help students prepare for their oral presentations
    3. To help students organize and review the information the found in the library

Activity #1
    Distribute Writing Assignment #1. Discuss the directions in detail and give students ample time to complete the assignment.

NOTE: Students may use this assignment to complete their Nonfiction Reading Assignment Sheet or they may wait until the assignment in Lesson Fifteen.

WRITING ASSIGNMENT #1 - *One Day in the Life of Ivan Denisovich*

PROMPT

You have had time to gather information and make notes about the topic you were assigned relating to Russia. Now you need to review that information and get ready for your oral report. Your assignment is to write a composition in which you summarize the most important information from your research.

PREWRITING

Most of your prewriting has been done. You have read lots of articles and parts of books and have taken notes of the most important information you have found. Now, organize your notes. You will probably find that different parts of your notes fall under the same categories or naturally relate to each other. Make a little list of the kinds of information you have found. Organize that list into an outline. Arrange your information in chronological order if possible. If your information does not fit into chronological order, find another method of organizing it that makes sense. Put background information first, if you have it. If your information falls into equal categories (such as kinds of transportation, branches of the military, or kinds of music, for example), arrange your information in a way that is most logical.

DRAFTING

Because your information is all different, giving specific instructions is difficult at best. You all should have an introductory paragraph in which you introduce the topic about which you are reporting. In the body of your compositions, you should have paragraphs with topic sentences telling what each paragraph is about, and then fill out the paragraphs with details and examples to explain or show your point. Finish with a concluding paragraph in which you give your conclusions about your topic.

PROMPT

When you finish the rough draft of your paper, ask a student who sits near you to read it. After reading your rough draft, he/she should tell you what he/she liked best about your work, which parts were difficult to understand, and ways in which your work could be improved. Reread your paper considering your critic's comments, and make the corrections you think are necessary.

PROOFREADING

Do a final proofreading of your paper double-checking your grammar, spelling, organization, and the clarity of your ideas.

LESSON THREE

Objectives
    1. To inform students about life in Russia
    2. To give students the opportunity to practice public speaking
    3. To conclude the research projects

Activity
    Use this class period for students to give their oral reports about the topics they have researched.

LESSON FOUR

Objectives
    1. To distribute the materials students will need to use in this unit
    2. To preview the study questions and vocabulary for Reading Assignment #1
    3. To read Reading Assignment #1

Activity #1
    Distribute the materials students will use in this unit. Explain in detail how students are to use these materials.

    Study Guides Students should read the study guide questions for each reading assignment prior to beginning the reading assignment to get a feeling for what events and ideas are important in the section they are about to read. After reading the section, students will (as a class or individually) answer the questions to review the important events and ideas from that section of the book. Students should keep the study guides as study materials for the unit test.

    Vocabulary Prior to reading a reading assignment, students will do vocabulary work related to the section of the book they are about to read. Following the completion of the reading of the book, there will be a vocabulary review of all the words used in the vocabulary assignments. Students should keep their vocabulary work as study materials for the unit test.

    Reading Assignment Sheet You need to fill in the reading assignment sheet to let students know by when their reading has to be completed. You can either write the assignment sheet up on a side blackboard or bulletin board and leave it there for students to see each day, or you can "ditto" copies for each student to have. In either case, you should advise students to become very familiar with the reading assignments so they know what is expected of them.

<u>Extra Activities Center</u>   The Unit Resource portion of this unit contains suggestions for an extra library of related books and articles in your classroom as well as crossword and word search puzzles. Make an extra activities center in your room where you will keep these materials for students to use. (Bring the books and articles in from the library and keep several copies of the puzzles on hand.) Explain to students that these materials are available for students to use when they finish reading assignments or other class work early.

<u>Nonfiction Assignment Sheet</u>   Explain to students that they each are to read at least one non-fiction piece from the in-class library at some time during the unit. Students will fill out a nonfiction assignment sheet after completing the reading to help you evaluate their reading experiences and to help the students think about and evaluate their own reading experiences.

<u>Books</u>   Each school has its own rules and regulations regarding student use of school books. Advise students of the procedures that are normal for your school.

<u>Activity #3</u>
   Give students about 15 minutes to preview the study questions and have students do the vocabulary work for Reading Assignment #1 of *One Day In The Life of Ivan Denisovich*.

<u>Activity #4</u>
   Have students read Reading Assignment #1 of *One Day In The Life of Ivan Denisovich* out loud in class. You probably know the best way to get readers with your class; pick students at random, ask for volunteers, or use whatever method works best for your group. If you have not yet completed an oral reading evaluation for your students this marking period, this would be a good opportunity to do so. A form is included with this unit for your convenience.

   If students do not finish this assignment during this class period, they should complete it prior to the next class meeting.

NONFICTION ASSIGNMENT SHEET
(To be completed after reading the required nonfiction article)

Name _____ Date _____

Title of Nonfiction Read _____

Written By _____ Publication Date _____

I. Factual Summary: Write a short summary of the piece you read.

II. Vocabulary
    1. With which vocabulary words in the piece did you encounter some degree of difficulty?

    2. How did you resolve your lack of understanding with these words?

III. Interpretation: What was the main point the author wanted you to get from reading his work?

IV. Criticism
    1. With which points of the piece did you agree or find easy to accept? Why?

    2. With which points of the piece did you disagree or find difficult to believe? Why?

V. Personal Response: What do you think about this piece? OR How does this piece influence your ideas?

LESSON FIVE

Objectives
1. To review the main events and ideas from Reading Assignment #1
2. To preview the study questions for Reading Assignment #2
3. To familiarize students with the vocabulary in Reading Assignment #2
4. To read Reading Assignment #2

Activity #1

Give students a few minutes to formulate answers for the study guide questions for Reading Assignment #1, and then discuss the answers to the questions in detail. Write the answers on the board or overhead transparency so students can have the correct answers for study purposes. Note: It is a good practice in public speaking and leadership skills for individual students to take charge of leading the discussions of the study questions. Perhaps a different student could go to the front of the class and lead the discussion each day that the study questions are discussed during this unit. Of course, the teacher should guide the discussion when appropriate and be sure to fill in any gaps the students leave.

Activity #2

Give students about fifteen minutes to preview the study questions for Reading Assignment #2 of *One Day In The Life of Ivan Denisovich* and to do the related vocabulary work.

Activity #3

Assign students to read Reading Assignment #2 of *One Day In The Life of Ivan Denisovich* prior to your next class period. If there is time remaining in this period, students may begin reading silently.

ORAL READING EVALUATION - *Ivan Denisovich*

Name _____ Class____ Date _____

SKILL	EXCELLENT	GOOD	AVERAGE	FAIR	POOR
Fluency	5	4	3	2	1
Clarity	5	4	3	2	1
Audibility	5	4	3	2	1
Pronunciation	5	4	3	2	1
_____	5	4	3	2	1
_____	5	4	3	2	1

Total _____ Grade _____

Comments:

LESSON SIX

Objectives
1. To check to see that students read Reading Assignment #2 as assigned
2. To review the main ideas and events from Reading Assignment #2
3. To preview the study questions for Reading Assignment #3
4. To familiarize students with the vocabulary in Reading Assignment #3
5. To read Reading Assignment #3
6. To give students the opportunity to practice writing to express their own personal opinions
7. To break up the read-and-question routine

Activity #1

Quiz - Distribute quizzes and give students about 10 minutes to complete them. (Note: The quizzes may either be the short answer study guides or the multiple choice version for Reading Assignment #2.) Have students exchange papers. Grade the quizzes as a class. Collect the papers for recording the grades. (If you used the multiple choice version as a quiz, take a few minutes to discuss the answers for the short answer version if your students are using the short answer version for their study guides.)

Activity #2

Tell students that prior to your next class period, they should preview the study questions, do the related vocabulary work, and read Reading Assignment #3.

Activity #3

Distribute Writing Assignment #2. Discuss the directions in detail and give students ample time to complete the assignment. Be sure to tell students when the compositions will be due.

WRITING ASSIGNMENT #2 - *One Day in the Life of Ivan Denisovich*

PROMPT

You are reading a book that is basically just a description of the day in one man's life, yet it actually is a comment on a whole way of life, a whole country's system of government and justice.

Your assignment is to write a composition entitled, "One Day in the Life of <u>(Your Name)</u>. You may write it in one of any number of different styles--as an essay, a short story, a poem, lyrics to a ballad or rap music--, and you may use any point of view you choose--anything from first person narrative to even being a bug on your own shoulder as you go through your day!

Have fun, but also try your best to choose events and comments which also give your own commentary on your life.

PREWRITING

Make some notes about what kinds of events you will put into your day. Will you take an actual day you have lived or will you make a composite day that is representative of your life? What will you include.

Decide upon a form for your composition. Will you write a short story, lyrics, a poem--what?

Decide upon a point of view. How will you tell about your day?

Make a little outline to follow as you write.

DRAFTING

Following your outline, write your first draft. Rewrite and revise as necessary.

PROMPT

When you finish the rough draft of your paper to your own satisfaction, ask a student who sits near you to read it. After reading your rough draft, he/she should tell you what he/she liked best about your work, which parts were difficult to understand, and ways in which your work could be improved. Reread your paper considering your critic's comments, and make the corrections you think are necessary.

PROOFREADING

Do a final proofreading of your paper double-checking your grammar, spelling, organization, and the clarity of your ideas.

LESSON SEVEN

Objectives
1. To review the main ideas and events from Reading Assignment #3
2. To preview the study questions and vocabulary for Reading Assignment #4
3. To read Reading Assignment #4

Activity #1
Give students a few minutes to formulate answers to the study guide questions for Reading Assignment #3. Discuss the answers to the questions in detail.

Activity #2
Give students about fifteen minutes to preview the study questions and do the related vocabulary work for Reading Assignment #4.

Activity #3
If you have completed the oral reading evaluations, have students read Reading Assignment #4 silently. If you have not yet completed the oral reading evaluations, use this class period to do so.

If students do not complete Reading Assignment #4 in class, they should do so prior to the next class meeting.

LESSON EIGHT

Objectives
1. To review the main events of Reading Assignment #4
2. To assign the pre-reading, vocabulary and reading work for Reading Assignment #5
3. To give the teacher time to talk with students about their writing skills

Activity #1

Give students a few minutes to formulate answers to the study guide questions for Reading Assignment #4. Discuss the answers to the questions in detail.

Activity #2

Give students about ten minutes to do the prereading work for Reading Assignment #5.

Activity #3

Tell students that prior to the next period they should have completed reading *One Day In The Life of Ivan Denisovich*. Give students this class period to read Reading Assignment #5 silently to complete reading the book. If students do not finish this assignment in class, they should do so prior to the next class meeting.

Activity #4

While students are reading, call students to your desk (or some other private area) to discuss their papers from Writing Assignment 1. A Writing Evaluation Form is included with this unit to help structure your conferences.

WRITING EVALUATION FORM - *One Day In The Life of Ivan Denisovich*

Name _____ Date _____

      Grade _____

Circle One For Each Item:

Grammar:	excellent	good	fair	poor
Spelling:	excellent	good	fair	poor
Punctuation:	excellent	good	fair	poor
Legibility:	excellent	good	fair	poor

Strengths:

Weaknesses:

Comments/Suggestions:

LESSONS NINE AND TEN

Objectives
    1. To review the main events and ideas from Reading Assignment #5
    2. To discuss *One Day In The Life of Ivan Denisovich* on interpretive and critical levels

Activity #1
    Give students a few minutes to formulate answers to the study questions for Reading Assignment #5. Discuss the answers to the questions in detail.

Activity #2
    Assign one of the Extra Discussion Questions/Writing Assignments to each of your students. Advise students that they will be responsible for leading a class discussion about the questions they have been assigned. Give students ample time to prepare their answers.

Activity #3
    Have each student lead a discussion he/she was assigned. Use these responses as springboards for class discussions of the topics suggested by the questions. Jump in as necessary to guide the discussion and to add important points the students may have missed.

NOTE: Since there are so many discussion questions and since some of the topics involved may take a substantial amount of time to discuss in depth, allow an additional class period for this activity.

EXTRA WRITING ASSIGNMENTS/DISCUSSION QUESTIONS - *Ivan Denisovich*

Interpretation

1. From what point of view is *Ivan Denisovich* written, and what effect does that have on the story?

2. Is the story of *Ivan Denisovich* believable? Explain why or why not.

3. Is there a climax in the story? Explain.

4. Are the characters in *Ivan Denisovich* stereotypes? If so, explain the usefulness of employing stereotypes in the novel. If they are not, explain how they merit individuality.

5. What is the setting of the story? Could this story have been set in a different time and place and still have the same effect?

6. What are the conflicts in the story? Are the conflicts all resolved? If so, how? If not, why not?

7. Divide *Ivan Denisovich* into chapters and title each chapter. Justify your choices.

Critical

8. Compare and contrast Ivan Denisovich and Fetiukov.

9. Compare and contrast Ivan and Alyosha.

10. Characterize Alexander Solzhenitsyn's style of writing. How does it contribute to the value of the novel?

11. Explain why Ivan's unit works so hard together on the block walls.

12. Explain the impact of Article 58 of the Criminal Code on each of the prisoners in Ivan's unit.

13. Discuss the use and value of bribes in the "special" prison.

14. In what ways is Ivan shown as a human being instead of a perfect hero? Where do some of his flaws show up? Give examples.

15. Give several examples of Solzhenitsyn's use of understatement in the story and explain its effect.

Ivan Denisovich Extra Discussion Questions page 2

16. What faults in his society does Alexander Solzhenitsyn point out in *Ivan Denisovich*?

17. "Thank God for the man who does his job and keeps his mouth shut!" Why?

18. "It's no joke to rob 500 men of over half an hour." Why was that half hour so important to the men? (One might think time would be irrelevant in prison.)

19. Can the prisoners survive without taking risks?

20. It was said on several occasions that no one ever escaped and no one had ever finished his sentence. What kept the prisoners going with their daily routine even though they knew these facts?

Personal Response

21. Did you enjoy reading *Ivan Denisovich*? Why or why not?

22. Are there any circumstances under which it would be right to give or receive bribes in our society today? Are there people who do it? If so, who are they?

23. How important is luck in a prisoner's survival?

24. How important are having luck and taking risks in our society today?

25. Does anyone have control over his own destiny? Explain.

26. Ivan had a "code" by which he lived. What is your code?

27. Ivan had certain techniques by which he survived in prison. Are there any "techniques" to surviving in our society? If so, what are they? If not, why not?

28. Have you read any other books or seen any other stories like *One Day in the Life of Ivan Denisovich*? If so, what were they. If not, why do you suppose you haven't?

LESSON ELEVEN

Objective
    To review all of the vocabulary work done in this unit

Activity
    Choose one (or more) of the vocabulary review activities listed below and spend your class period as directed in the activity. Some of the materials for these review activities are located in the Vocabulary Resource section in this unit.

VOCABULARY REVIEW ACTIVITIES

1. Divide your class into two teams and have an old-fashioned spelling or definition bee.

2. Give each of your students (or students in groups of two, three or four) a *One Day In The Life of Ivan Denisovich* Vocabulary Word Search Puzzle. The person (group) to find all of the vocabulary words in the puzzle first wins.

3. Give students a *One Day In The Life of Ivan Denisovich* Vocabulary Word Search Puzzle without the word list. The person or group to find the most vocabulary words in the puzzle wins.

4. Use a *One Day In The Life of Ivan Denisovich* Vocabulary Crossword Puzzle. Put the puzzle onto a transparency on the overhead projector (so everyone can see it), and do the puzzle together as a class.

5. Give students a *One Day In The Life of Ivan Denisovich* Vocabulary Matching Worksheet to do.

6. Divide your class into two teams. Use the *Ivan Denisovich* vocabulary words with their letters jumbled as a word list. Student 1 from Team A faces off against Student 1 from Team B. You write the first jumbled word on the board. The first student (1A or 1B) to unscramble the word wins the chance for his/her team to score points. If 1A wins the jumble, go to student 2A and give him/her a definition. He/she must give you the correct spelling of the vocabulary word which fits that definition. If he/she does, Team A scores a point, and you give student 3A a definition for which you expect a correctly spelled matching vocabulary word. Continue giving Team A definitions until some team member makes an incorrect response. An incorrect response sends the game back to the jumbled-word face off, this time with students 2A and 2B. Instead of repeating giving definitions to the first few students of each team, continue with the student after the one who gave the last incorrect response on the team. For example, if Team B wins the jumbled-word face-off, and student 5B gave the last incorrect answer for Team B, you would start this round of definition questions with student 6B, and so on. The team with the most points wins!

7. Have students write a story in which they correctly use as many vocabulary words as possible. Have students read their compositions orally! Post the most original compositions on your bulletin board!

LESSONS TWELVE AND THIRTEEN

Objectives
1. To further study the ideas presented in *One Day In The Life of Ivan Denisovich*
2. To give students the opportunity to practice working together in small groups
3. To help students review the text and find important ideas they may have missed on the first reading
4. To give students the opportunity to practice their public speaking skills

Activity #1
Divide your class into 9 groups -- one group for each of the following topics:

1. Point of view
2. Religion
3. Types of prisoners
4. Ivan's code for living
5. Importance of food
6. Importance of work
7. Survival techniques
8. Symbolism
9. The message of the book

Allow the groups time to find relevant passages relating to their topics. Allow time for the group members to discuss their findings and come up with some intelligent statements about their findings. The groups should appoint one spokesperson to report the group's findings and conclusions.

Activity #2
Call on groups to give their information. Use the groups' reports as springboards for discussions of the topics. Jot their ideas down briefly on the board for students to copy into their notes. Allow time for discussion and questions about each point. Be sure to add anything important the the groups might miss.

LESSON FOURTEEN

Objectives
1. To give students the opportunity to practice writing to persuade
2. To review the main ideas in the novel
3. To give the teacher the opportunity to evaluate students' writing skills

Activity
Distribute Writing Assignment #3. Discuss the directions in detail and give students ample time to complete the assignment. Tell students when their compositions will be due.

LESSON FIFTEEN

Objective
To familiarize students with how our criminal justice system works

Activity
Invite a local attorney or judge to come to your class to explain to your students how our criminal justice system works. Have the attorney explain a person's rights and the responsibilities of the criminal justice system. Also have your guest speaker explain exactly what it is like in jail and what kinds of work programs prisoners may have. A few words about the strengths and weaknesses and current issues facing our criminal justice system would also be appropriate. Give students the chance to ask any questions they may have.

LESSON SIXTEEN

Objectives
1. To give students the opportunity to read different points of view about some of the things they were told by the guest speaker
2. To give the students the opportunity to study a little more closely the current issues facing our criminal justice system

Activity
Take students to the library. Their assignment is to read at least two articles that relate to our criminal justice system. Students should take notes, so they can relate the specifics of their research to the class in the next class period.

LESSON SEVENTEEN

<u>Objectives</u>

    1. To expose all students to the combined wealth of information the whole class has read

    2. To further discuss the current issues relating to our criminal justice system

<u>Activity</u>

    Start with any student and have that student give a summary of his/her reading. Ask if anyone else read anything related to this topic. Have each of those students give the information they found. When that topic is concluded, pick another student and repeat the process until all students have had the opportunity to tell about what they read.

WRITING ASSIGNMENT #3 - *One Day in the Life of Ivan Denisovich*

PROMPT

If we find unfair or bad conditions in our country, we have ways of working to improve those conditions. We can make a petition, write letters of complaint, notify various government agencies, go on strike, or any of several other options. All countries aren't like that. In some countries, people have no way of improving their situations. In fact, often complaints bring down only worse conditions as a punishment for complaining.

Since you live in a democracy, you should learn how to write a letter persuading someone to improve conditions or to amend a policy. Your assignment is to write such a letter about the topic of your choice. If you can't think of anything to write about, pretend you are Ivan Denisovich writing a letter to improve conditions at the work camp.

PREWRITING

Is everything in the world just the way you think it should be? Think about your own life at school, at home, at work (if you have a job). Are you satisfied with all aspects of each environment? If not, write down one specific problem that exists that you would like to have changed. Write down two reasons why the problem should be changed. Next to each reason, jot down a couple of specific examples to illustrate your point. Write down to what the problem should be changed. What is the solution, the improvement, the better way? Write down at least two reasons why this way is better. Next to each reason, jot down a couple of specific examples to illustrate your point.

DRAFTING

Write a paragraph in which you introduce the problem.

In the body of your composition, write two paragraphs telling why the problem should be changed, one paragraph for each reason you jotted down in the prewriting stage. Fill out each paragraph with the specific examples you jotted down next to the reasons.

Following that in the body of your paragraph, write a paragraph telling to what the problem should be changed--give your solution.

Follow your solution with two paragraphs explaining why your solution is better than the current situation, one paragraph for each of the reasons you stated in the prewriting stage. Fill out your paragraphs with specific examples.

End your composition with a concluding paragraph in which you summarize your main points and close your arguments.

PROOFREADING

When you finish the rough draft of your paper to your own satisfaction, ask a student who sits near you to read it. After reading your rough draft, he/she should tell you what he/she liked best about your work, which parts were difficult to understand, and ways in which your work could be improved. Reread your paper considering your critic's comments, and make the corrections you think are necessary.

LESSON EIGHTEEN

Objective
   To review the main ideas presented in *One Day In The Life of Ivan Denisovich*

Activity #1
   Choose one of the review games/activities included in this unit and spend your class period as outlined there. Some materials for these activities are located in the Extra Activities section of this unit.

Activity #2
   Remind students that the Unit Test will be in the next class meeting. Stress the review of the Study Guides and their class notes as a last minute, brush-up review for homework.

REVIEW GAMES/ACTIVITIES - *One Day In The Life of Ivan Denisovich*

1. Ask the class to make up a unit test for *One Day In The Life of Ivan Denisovich*. The test should have 4 sections: matching, true/false, short answer, and essay. Students may use 1/2 period to make the test and then swap papers and use the other 1/2 class period to take a test a classmate has devised. (open book) You may want to use the unit test included in this guide or take questions from the students' unit tests to formulate your own test.

2. Take 1/2 period for students to make up true and false questions (including the answers). Collect the papers and divide the class into two teams. Draw a big tic-tac-toe board on the chalk board. Make one team X and one team O. Ask questions to each side, giving each student one turn. If the question is answered correctly, that students' team's letter (X or O) is placed in the box. If the answer is incorrect, no mark is placed in the box. The object is to get three marks in a row like tic-tac-toe. You may want to keep track of the number of games won for each team.

3. Take 1/2 period for students to make up questions (true/false and short answer). Collect the questions. Divide the class into two teams. You'll alternate asking questions to individual members of teams A & B (like in a spelling bee). The question keeps going from A to B until it is correctly answered, then a new question is asked. A correct answer does not allow the team to get another question. Correct answers are +2 points; incorrect answers are -1 point.

4. Have students pair up and quiz each other from their study guides and class notes.

5. Give students a *One Day In The Life of Ivan Denisovich* crossword puzzle to complete.

6. Divide your class into two teams. Use the *Ivan Denisovich* crossword words with their letters jumbled as a word list. Student 1 from Team A faces off against Student 1 from Team B. You write the first jumbled word on the board. The first student (1A or 1B) to unscramble the word wins the chance for his/her team to score points. If 1A wins the jumble, go to student 2A and give him/her a clue. He/she must give you the correct word which matches that clue. If he/she does, Team A scores a point, and you give student 3A a clue for which you expect another correct response. Continue giving Team A clues until some team member makes an incorrect response. An incorrect response sends the game back to the jumbled-word face off, this time with students 2A and 2B. Instead of repeating giving clues to the first few students of each team, continue with the student after the one who gave the last incorrect response on the team. For example, if Team B wins the jumbled-word face-off, and student 5B gave the last incorrect answer for Team B, you would start this round of clue questions with student 6B, and so on. The team with the most points wins!

UNIT TESTS

SHORT ANSWER UNIT TEST 1 - *One Day In The Life of Ivan Denisovich*

I. Matching

___ 1. Shukhov   A. Winter shoes

___ 2. Solzhenitsyn   B. Construction foreman

___ 3. Valenki   C. The Baptist

___ 4. Tartar   D. Assistant squad leader

___ 5. Pavlo   E. Missing prisoner

___ 6. Alyosha   F. The author

___ 7. Volkovoy   G. Scavenger

___ 8. Kasha   H. Captain

___ 9. Der   I. Ivan Denisovich

___ 10. Senka   J. Oatmeal-type food

___ 11. Markovich   K. Ivan's wife

___ 12. Tiurin   L. Had been to Buchenwald

___ 13. Fetiukov   M. Mason who worked with Ivan

___ 14. Kilgas   N. In charge of discipline

___ 15. Buinovsky   O. Prison Guard

                        P. Gets many parcels

                        Q. Gang boss

Denisovich Short Answer Unit Test 1 Page 2

II. Short Answer

1. The Tartar sentenced Ivan to three days penalty with work for oversleeping. How did Ivan get out of serving his sentence?

2. Ivan did a lousy job of washing the guardroom floor. Why?

3. How did the 104th get out of being sent to the Socialist Way of Life settlement to work?

4. Why didn't Ivan want to be a carpet painter after his release?

5. Why were snowstorms both a blessing and a curse to the prisoners?

6. What kind of work did Fetiukov and the captain have? Why was that ironic?

Denisovich Short Answer Unit Test 1 Page 3

7. Why did the men often have short rations?

8. Why did Ivan keep working after it was time to stop?

9. How did the 104th exert its independence on the way back from work?

10. What was Ivan's reward for holding a place in line for Tsezar?

III. Composition
   What is the point of *One Day In The Life of Ivan Denisovich*? When we read books, we usually come away from our reading experience a little richer, having given more thought to a particular aspect of life. What do you think Alexander Solzhenitsyn intended us to gain from reading his novel?

Denisovich Short Answer Unit Test 1 Page 4

IV. Vocabulary

Listen to the vocabulary words and write them down. Go back later and fill in the correct definition for each word.

1.

2.

3.

4.

5.

6.

7.

8.

9.

10.

KEY: SHORT ANSWER UNIT TEST #1 - *One Day In The Life of Ivan Denisovich*

I. Matching/Identify

_I_	1. Shukhov		A. Winter shoes
_F_	2. Solzhenitsyn		B. Construction foreman
_A_	3. Valenki		C. The Baptist
_O_	4. Tartar		D. Assistant squad leader
_D_	5. Pavlo		E. Missing prisoner
_C_	6. Alyosha		F. The author
_N_	7. Volkovoy		G. Scavenger
_J_	8. Kasha		H. Captain
_B_	9. Der		I. Ivan Denisovich
_L_	10. Senka		J. Oatmeal-type food
_P_	11. Markovich		K. Ivan's wife
_Q_	12. Tiurin		L. Had been to Buchenwald
_G_	13. Fetiukov		M. Mason who worked with Ivan
_M_	14. Kilgas		N. In charge of discipline
_H_	15. Buinovsky		O. Prison Guard
			P. Gets many parcels
			Q. Gang boss

II. Short Answer

1. The Tartar sentenced Ivan to three days penalty with work for oversleeping. How did Ivan get out of serving his sentence?
    The Tartar really only wanted someone to clean the guardroom floor, so he gave Ivan that assignment and let the sentence go.

2. Ivan did a lousy job of washing the guardroom floor. Why?
    "When you worked for the knowing you gave them quality; when you worked for a fool you simply gave him eyewash."

3. How did the 104th get out of being sent to the Socialist Way of Life settlement to work?
    The squad leader, Tiurin, had bribed the officials at the planning department with salt pork.

4. Why didn't Ivan want to be a carpet painter after his release?
    He didn't think it was an honest profession like carpentry or plumbing. "Easy money weighs light in the hand and doesn't give you the feeling you've earned it."

5. Why were snowstorms both a blessing and a curse to the prisoners?
    They got off of work for those days but had to make them up by working Sundays.

6. What kind of work did Fetiukov and the captain have? Why was that ironic?
    They were both in positions of responsibility in the outside world, but in the camp they were doing labor, bringing up loads of sand. Ivan was just an average man but was given responsible jobs as one of the best prison workers. The standard in prison was different from the outside world; roles were reversed.

7. Why did the men often have short rations?
    The cook paid his helpers with extra portions of food. Since the cook was lazy, he had a lot of people to pay and the men often had short rations.

8. Why did Ivan keep working after it was time to stop?
    There was mortar left, which would freeze and be useless if it wasn't used up. He worried about anything he could make use of, about every scrap of work he could do -- nothing must be wasted without good reason.

9. How did the 104th exert its independence on the way back from work?
    They ignored the guards telling them to hurry up. Yet, when they decided to "race" the column from the machine works, they all ran without the guards' command to do so.

10. What was Ivan's reward for holding a place in line for Tsezar?
    Tsezar gave him his dinner portion and bread.

III. Composition   Answers will vary.
    What is the point of *One Day In The Life of Ivan Denisovich*? When we read books, we usually come away from our reading experience a little richer, having given more thought to a particular aspect of life. What do you think Alexander Solzhenitsyn intended us to gain from reading his novel?

IV. Vocabulary
    Choose ten of the vocabulary words. Read them orally to your class so the students can write them down on part IV of their vocabulary tests.

SHORT ANSWER UNIT TEST 2 - *One Day In The Life of Ivan Denisovich*

I. Matching

___ 1. Shukhov   A. The author

___ 2. Solzhenitsyn   B. Ivan Denisovich

___ 3. Valenki   C. Oatmeal-type food

___ 4. Tartar   D. Ivan's wife

___ 5. Pavlo   E. Captain

___ 6. Alyosha   F. Winter shoes

___ 7. Volkovoy   G. Scavenger

___ 8. Kasha   H. Missing prisoner

___ 9. Der   I. Gang boss

___ 10. Senka   J. The Baptist

___ 11. Markovich   K. Gets many parcels

___ 12. Tiurin   L. In charge of discipline

___ 13. Fetiukov   M. Prison Guard

___ 14. Kilgas   N. Had been to Buchenwald

___ 15. Buinovsky   O. Mason who worked with Ivan

                                                                          P. Assistant squad leader

                                                                          Q. Construction foreman

Denisovich Short Answer Unit Test 2 Page 2

II. Short Answer

1. "The thoughts of a prisoner -- they're not free either." Why not?

2. "That wasn't the way to eat, he learned in camp. You had to eat with all of your mind on the food ---." Why did Ivan think that?

3. The experienced prisoners get by by stashing useful things and economizing. Give at least four examples.

4. Why did Ivan like to work?

5. What kind of work did Fetiukov and the captain have? Why was that ironic?

6. What were the circumstances leading to Ivan's incarceration?

7. The idea that the squad works together for mutual benefit or honor is shown several times. Give at least two examples.

Denisovich Short Answer Unit Test 2 Page 3

8. Why was Alyosha glad to be in prison?

9. What was Ivan's view of religion?

10. What strokes of luck had Ivan had that day?

III. Composition

One Day in the Life of Ivan Denisovich has been called "a brutally graphic picture of life in a Stalinist work camp and a moving tribute to man's will to prevail over relentless dehumanization." Defend that statement using specific examples from the text.

Denisovich Short Answer Unit Test 2 Page 4

IV. Vocabulary

Listen to the vocabulary words and write them down. Go back later and fill in the correct definition for each word.

1.

2.

3.

4.

5.

6.

7.

8.

9.

10.

KEY: SHORT ANSWER UNIT TEST 2 *One Day In The Life of Ivan Denisovich*

I. Matching (Use this matching key also for the Advanced Short Answer Unit Test)

_B_	1. Shukhov	A.	The author
_A_	2. Solzhenitsyn	B.	Ivan Denisovich
_F_	3. Valenki	C.	Oatmeal-type food
_M_	4. Tartar	D.	Ivan's wife
_P_	5. Pavlo	E.	Captain
_J_	6. Alyosha	F.	Winter shoes
_L_	7. Volkovoy	G.	Scavenger
_C_	8. Kasha	H.	Missing prisoner
_Q_	9. Der	I.	Gang boss
_N_	10. Senka	J.	The Baptist
_K_	11. Markovich	K.	Gets many parcels
_I_	12. Tiurin	L.	In charge of discipline
_G_	13. Fetiukov	M.	Prison Guard
_O_	14. Kilgas	N.	Had been to Buchenwald
_E_	15. Buinovsky	O.	Mason who worked with Ivan
		P.	Assistant squad leader
		Q.	Construction foreman

II. Short Answer

1. "The thoughts of a prisoner -- they're not free either." Why not?
   "They kept returning to the same things." (food, warmth, fate of self and fellow prisoners)

2. "That wasn't the way to eat, he learned in camp. You had to eat with all of your mind on the food ---." Why did Ivan think that?
   He considered the large amount of work he had done while in the camp eating a small amount of food (rather than always being full).

3. The experienced prisoners get by by stashing useful things and economizing. Give at least four examples.
   bread -- trowel -- roll of roofing felt -- hacksaw blade

4. Why did Ivan like to work?
   It made time go fast, made him forget his troubles and worries, and it gave him something he could be proud of.

5. What kind of work did Fetiukov and the captain have? Why was that ironic?
   They were both in positions of responsibility in the outside world, but in camp they were doing labor, bringing up loads of sand. Ivan was just an average man but was given responsible jobs as one of the best workers at the camp. Their roles were reversed.

6. What were the circumstances leading to Ivan's incarceration?
   He was sentenced for high treason. He had agreed to carry out a mission for German intelligence. He had a choice of carrying out the mission or being killed, so he agreed to carry out the mission.

7. The idea that the squad works together for mutual benefit or honor is shown several times. Give at least two examples.
   -- All going to work early after lunch
   -- All running in for the evening (to beat the other squad)
   -- Mortar men keeping up with masons

8. Why was Alyosha glad to be in prison?
   "Here you have time to think about your soul."

9. What was Ivan's view of religion?
   "I'm not against God, understand that. I do believe in God. But I don't believe in paradise or in hell. . . . somehow it works out all right for you [Alyosha]: Jesus Christ wanted you to sit in prison and so you are -- sitting there for His sake. But for whose sake am I here?"

10. What strokes of luck had Ivan had that day?

"He'd had many strokes of luck that day: they hadn't put him in the cells; they hadn't sent his squad to the settlement; he'd swiped a bowl of kasha at dinner; the squad leader had fixed the rates well; he'd built a wall and enjoyed doing it; he's smuggled that bit of hacksaw blade through; he'd earned a favor from Tsezar that evening; he'd bought that tobacco. And he hadn't fallen ill."

IV. Vocabulary

Choose ten of the vocabulary words and read them orally to your class so students can write them down.

ADVANCED SHORT ANSWER UNIT TEST - *One Day In The Life of Ivan Denisovich*

I. Matching/Identify

___ 1. Shukhov   A. The author

___ 2. Solzhenitsyn   B. Ivan Denisovich

___ 3. Valenki   C. Oatmeal-type food

___ 4. Tartar   D. Ivan's wife

___ 5. Pavlo   E. Captain

___ 6. Alyosha   F. Winter shoes

___ 7. Volkovoy   G. Scavenger

___ 8. Kasha   H. Missing prisoner

___ 9. Der   I. Gang boss

___ 10. Senka   J. The Baptist

___ 11. Markovich   K. Gets many parcels

___ 12. Tiurin   L. In charge of discipline

___ 13. Fetiukov   M. Prison Guard

___ 14. Kilgas   N. Had been to Buchenwald

___ 15. Buinovsky   O. Mason who worked with Ivan

                                   P. Assistant squad leader

                                   Q. Construction foreman

Denisovich Advanced Short Answer Unit Test Page 2

II. Short Answer

1. Compare and contrast Ivan Denisovich and Fetiukov.

2. Compare and contrast Ivan and Alyosha.

3. Give at least three examples of the use of bribes in *Ivan Denisovich* and explain the value of the bribing system in the work camp.

4. Ivan Denisovich had a code by which he lived. Describe it.

Denisovich Advanced Short Answer Unit Test Page 3

5. "Real jail was when you were kept back from work." Explain.

6.   "The sun has already reached its peak," he announced.
   "If it's reached its peak," said the captain reflectively, "it's one o'clock, not noon."
   "What do you mean?" Shukhov demurred. "Every old-timer knows that the sun stands highest at dinner time."
   "Old timers, maybe," snapped the captain. "But since their day a new decree has been passed, and now the sun stands highest at one."
   "Who passed that decree?"
   "Soviet power."

   Explain the relevance of this passage.

7. It was said on several occasions that no one had ever escaped and no one had ever finished his sentence. What kept the prisoners going with their daily routine even though they knew those facts?

Denisovich Advanced Short Answer Unit Test Page 4

III. Composition

    Marvin L. Kalb said, ". . . Ivan Denisovich Shukhov was quickly recognized throughout the country as a touching symbol of the suffering which the Russian people had endured under the Stalinist system." Explain how Ivan Denisovich was such a symbol using specific examples from the text.

Denisovich Advanced Short Answer Unit Test Page 5

III. Vocabulary

Write down the vocabulary words you are given. Go back later and use all of those vocabulary words in a composition relating to *One Day In The Life of Ivan Denisovich*.

MULTIPLE CHOICE UNIT TEST 1 - *ONE DAY IN THE LIFE OF IVAN DENISOVICH*

I. Matching/Identify

___ 1. Shukhov   A. Winter shoes

___ 2. Solzhenitsyn   B. Construction foreman

___ 3. Valenki   C. The Baptist

___ 4. Tartar   D. Assistant squad leader

___ 5. Pavlo   E. Missing prisoner

___ 6. Alyosha   F. The author

___ 7. Volkovoy   G. Scavenger

___ 8. Kasha   H. Captain

___ 9. Der   I. Ivan Denisovich

___ 10. Senka   J. Oatmeal-type food

___ 11. Markovich   K. Ivan's wife

___ 12. Tiurin   L. Had been to Buchenwald

___ 13. Fetiukov   M. Mason who worked with Ivan

___ 14. Kilgas   N. In charge of discipline

___ 15. Buinovsky   O. Prison Guard

                                                         P. Gets many parcels

                                                         Q. Gang boss

Denisovich Multiple Choice Unit Test 1 Page 2

II. Multiple Choice

1. How did the 104th get out of being sent to the "Socialist Way of Life Settlement" to work?
    a. One of their squad members wrestled with a member of the other squad. The loser's squad, was sent to the settlement. Ivan's squad won.
    b. They traded two pairs of valenkis for the privilege of staying behind.
    c. They squad leader had bribed the officials at the planning department with salt pork.
    d. They simply refused to go. They decided they would rather take a punishment. In frustration, the guards sent another squad.

2. "The thoughts of a prisoner--they're not free either." Why not?
    a. The prisoners are occasionally sent to a reformation camp where they are brainwashed.
    b. They kept returning to the same things.
    c. The prisoners are drilled with the maxims of the State.
    d. After a long time in the camp, one's thoughts become empty and meaningless.

3. Which of the following statements tells what Ivan thought about food?
    a. Since the food was so bad and scarce, it was best to think of other things while eating.
    b. You should eat with all of your mind on the food.
    c. He thought it was sacred.
    d. He thought of it only as money; something with which to barter.

4. They experienced prisoners get by by stashing useful things and economizing. Which of the following is not one of the items they horde?
    a. Spoons
    b. Bread
    c. Trowel
    d. Hacksaw blade

5. How did Ivan feel about work?
    a. He liked it. It made time go fast and he forgot his troubles and worries. It gave him something to be proud of.
    b. He hated it. He resented working without pay.
    c. It was better than sitting in a cell all day, but not something he ever enjoyed.
    d. He would do anything to be able to stay away from work--even pretend to be sick.

Denisovich Multiple Choice Unit Test 1 Page 3

6. Fetiukov and the captain had positions of responsibility in the outside world, but in camp they were doing labor. Ivan was just an average man but was given responsible jobs as one of the best workers in the camp. What is this literary devise called?
    a. Reversibility
    b. Irony
    c. Metamorphosis
    d. Sarcasm

7. What did Ivan tell Kilgas about his 25 year sentence?
    a. Live for now, do the best you can, and the future will take care of itself.
    b. Plan for the future. It will take your mind off of the daily drudgery.
    c. The time would go by quickly.
    d. He would probably only have to serve about twelve years if he behaved and bribed the right people.

8. What were the circumstances leading to Ivan's incarceration?
    a. He had murdered a member of the police force during a riot.
    b. He was trying to defect to the United States. Someone informed on him, and he was imprisoned.
    c. He was accused of writing and distributing subversive literature to members of the army and to the general populace.
    d. He was a member of the Soviet army. His squad had been captured by the Germans, but he and a few others had escaped. When they made it back to their own lives, their story was not believed. They were accused of collaborating with the Germans.

9. Why did the men often have short rations?
    a. The officials frequently starved the prisoners out of their own sadistic impulses.
    b. Gas was in short supply and the food delivery trucks could not always deliver on schedule.
    c. There simply wasn't enough food in the country, and the politicians and military personnel were fed first.
    d. The cook paid his many helpers with extra portions of food.

10. The idea that the squad worked together for mutual benefit or honor is shown several times. Which of these is not an example?
    a. Sharing food packages.
    b. All going to work early after lunch.
    c. All running in for the evening to beat the other squad.
    d. Mortar men keeping up with Masons.

Denisovich Multiple Choice Unit Test 1 Page 3

11. Why did Ivan keep working after it was time to quit?
    a. He was trying to earn extra bread.
    b. He had asked for a few hours off for the following day. The squad leader agreed, but he had to make the time up ahead of time.
    c. There was mortar left, and he wanted to use it up before it froze.
    d. He was obsessed with working, because it kept his mind off his loneliness.

12. Why was Alyosha glad to be in prison?
    a. He had no family and few friends. At least in prison he had company.
    b. He had taken his son's place in prison. He was glad to make the sacrifice so his son could be free.
    c. He enjoyed having the time to think about his soul.
    d. He was mentally unstable. He truly believed that he had committed a crime against the state, and deserved to be punished.

13. What was Ivan's view of religion?
    a. He didn't believe in God at all. He said that if there were a God, there would be no wars or prisons.
    b. He was a devout man who believed wholeheartedly and prayed every day.
    c. He had, at one time, believed in God. Now he was not sure.
    d. He believed in God, but not in paradise or in hell.

14. When Ivan was falling asleep, he thought of the strokes of luck he had had that day. Which of the following was not one of his strokes of luck?
    a. He was first in line at mealtime.
    b. He had enjoyed building the wall.
    c. He had smuggled the bit of hacksaw blade through.
    d. He had been healthy.

III. Make a list of at least five points Alexander Solzhenitsyn makes in *Ivan Denisovich*.

Denisovich Multiple Choice Unit Test 1 Page 4

IV. Vocabulary

___ 1. Allocating   a. A controlled change in movement, direction or position ___

___ 2. Impractical   b. Not practical in nature; can't see or implement useful ideas

___ 3. Inert   c. Cut short

___ 4. Advocated   d. Unshakably calm and collected

___ 5. Contingency   e. Overbearing pride

___ 6. Twinge   f. Zest; energy

___ 7. Maneuver   g. Tight; in shape; tense

___ 8. Taut   h. Spoiled; gone bad

___ 9. Rancid   i. The art of subtlety and deceptiveness

___ 10. Intermittent   j. Ridiculing; jeering at; making fun of

___ 11. Arrogance   k. Stopping and starting at intervals

___ 12. Cunning   l. To make a summoning gesture

___ 13. Fury   m. Unable to move or act

___ 14. Mockery   n. Rage; anger

___ 15. Imperturbable   o. A possibility that must be prepared for

___ 16. Zeal   p. Gaining possession of

___ 17. Curtailed   q. Supported the cause or idea of something

___ 18. Begrudge   r. Envy the possession or enjoyment of

___ 19. Beckon   s. Distributing according to a plan

___ 20. Acquiring   t. A sudden, sharp emotional or physical pain

MULTIPLE CHOICE UNIT TEST 2 - *One Day In The Life of Ivan Denisovich*

I. Matching

___ 1. Shukhov   A. The author

___ 2. Solzhenitsyn   B. Ivan Denisovich

___ 3. Valenki   C. Oatmeal-type food

___ 4. Tartar   D. Ivan's wife

___ 5. Pavlo   E. Captain

___ 6. Alyosha   F. Winter shoes

___ 7. Volkovoy   G. Scavenger

___ 8. Kasha   H. Missing prisoner

___ 9. Der   I. Gang boss

___ 10. Senka   J. The Baptist

___ 11. Markovich   K. Gets many parcels

___ 12. Tiurin   L. In charge of discipline

___ 13. Fetiukov   M. Prison Guard

___ 14. Kilgas   N. Had been to Buchenwald

___ 15. Buinovsky   O. Mason who worked with Ivan

                         P. Assistant squad leader

                         Q. Construction foreman

Denisovich Multiple Choice Unit Test 2 Page 2

II. Multiple Choice

1. How did the 104th get out of being sent to the "Socialist Way of Life Settlement" to work?
    a. One of their squad members wrestled with a member of the other squad. The loser's squad, was sent to the settlement. Ivan's squad won.
    b. They traded two pairs of valenkis for the privilege of staying behind.
    c. They simply refused to go. They decided they would rather take a punishment. In frustration, the guards sent another squad.
    d. They squad leader had bribed the officials at the planning department with salt pork.

2. "The thoughts of a prisoner--they're not free either." Why not?
    a. They kept returning to the same things.
    b. The prisoners are occasionally sent to a reformation camp where they are brainwashed.
    c. The prisoners are drilled with the maxims of the State.
    d. After a long time in the camp, one's thoughts become empty and meaningless.

3. Which of the following statements tells what Ivan thought about food?
    a. Since the food was so bad and scarce, it was best to think of other things while eating.
    b. He thought it was sacred.
    c. You should eat with all of your mind on the food.
    d. He thought of it only as money; something with which to barter.

4. They experienced prisoners get by by stashing useful things and economizing. Which of the following is not one of the items they horde?
    a. Hacksaw blade
    b. Bread
    c. Trowel
    d. Spoons

5. How did Ivan feel about work?
    a. He hated it. He resented working without pay.
    b. He liked it. It made time go fast and he forgot his troubles and worries. It gave him something to be proud of.
    c. It was better than sitting in a cell all day, but not something he ever enjoyed.
    d. He would do anything to be able to stay away from work--even pretend to be sick.

Denisovich Multiple Choice Unit Test 2 Page 3

6. Fetiukov and the captain had positions of responsibility in the outside world, but in camp they were doing labor. Ivan was just an average man but was given responsible jobs as one of the best workers in the camp. What is this literary devise called?
    a. Reversibility
    b. Metamorphosis
    c. Irony
    d. Sarcasm

7. What did Ivan tell Kilgas about his 25 year sentence?
    a. He would probably only have to serve about twelve years if he behaved and bribed the right people.
    b. Plan for the future. It will take your mind off of the daily drudgery.
    c. The time would go by quickly.
    d. Live for now, do the best you can, and the future will take care of itself.

8. What were the circumstances leading to Ivan's incarceration?
    a. He had murdered a member of the police force during a riot.
    b. He was a member of the Soviet army. His squad had been captured by the Germans, but he and a few others had escaped. When they made it back to their own lives, their story was not believed. They were accused of collaborating with the Germans.
    c. He was accused of writing and distributing subversive literature to members of the army and to the general populace.
    d. He was trying to defect to the United States. Someone informed on him, and he was imprisoned.

9. Why did the men often have short rations?
    a. The officials frequently starved the prisoners out of their own sadistic impulses.
    b. Gas was in short supply and the food delivery trucks could not always deliver on schedule.
    c. The cook paid his many helpers with extra portions of food.
    d. There simply wasn't enough food in the country, and the politicians and military personnel were fed first.

10. The idea that the squad worked together for mutual benefit or honor is shown several times. Which of these is not an example?
    a. All going to work early after lunch.
    b. Sharing food packages.
    c. All running in for the evening to beat the other squad.
    d. Mortar men keeping up with Masons.

Denisovich Multiple Choice Unit Test 2 Page 4

11. Why did Ivan keep working after it was time to quit?
    a. There was mortar left, and he wanted to use it up before it froze.
    b. He had asked for a few hours off for the following day. The squad leader agreed, but he had to make the time up ahead of time.
    c. He was trying to earn extra bread.
    d. He was obsessed with working, because it kept his mind off his loneliness.

12. Why was Alyosha glad to be in prison?
    a. He had no family and few friends. At least in prison he had company.
    b. He enjoyed having the time to think about his soul.
    c. He had taken his son's place in prison. He was glad to make the sacrifice so his son could be free.
    d. He was mentally unstable. He truly believed that he had committed a crime against the state, and deserved to be punished.

13. What was Ivan's view of religion?
    a. He didn't believe in God at all. He said that if there were a God, there would be no wars or prisons.
    b. He was a devout man who believed wholeheartedly and prayed every day.
    c. He believed in God, but not in paradise or in hell
    d. He had, at one time, believed in God. Now he was not sure.

14. When Ivan was falling asleep, he thought of the strokes of luck he had had that day. Which of the following was <u>not</u> one of his strokes of luck?
    a. He had been healthy.
    b. He had enjoyed building the wall.
    c. He had smuggled the bit of hacksaw blade through.
    d. He was first in line at mealtime.

III. Make a list of at least five points Alexander Solzhenitsyn makes in *Ivan Denisovich*.

Denisovich Multiple Choice Unit Test 1 Page 5

IV. Vocabulary

___ 1. Contingency   a. A sudden, sharp emotional or physical pain

___ 2. Zeal   b. Supported the cause or idea of something

___ 3. Arrogance   c. A possibility that must be prepared for

___ 4. Malicious   d. Ridiculing; jeering at; making fun of

___ 5. Mockery   e. Envy the possession or enjoyment of

___ 6. Consulting   f. Seeking advice or information from someone

___ 7. Curtailed   g. Devastatingly

___ 8. Advocated   h. Showing a desire to see others suffer

___ 9. Vicious   i. Not practical in nature; can't see or implement useful ideas

___ 10. Intermittent   j. Gaining possession of

___ 11. Impractical   k. Cut short

___ 12. Twinge   l. Savage; faulty; foul

___ 13. Maneuver   m. Spoiled; gone bad

___ 14. Ruse   n. Tight; in shape; tense

___ 15. Taut   o. Zest; energy

___ 16. Inert   p. Stopping and starting at intervals

___ 17. Acquiring   q. A crafty strategy; a diversion

___ 18. Witheringly   r. A controlled change in movement, direction or position

___ 19. Begrudge   s. Unable to move or act

___ 20. Rancid   t. Overbearing pride

ANSWER SHEET - *One Day In The Life of Ivan Denisovich*
Multiple Choice Unit Tests

I. Matching	II. Multiple Choice	IV. Vocabulary
1. ___	1. ___	1. ___
2. ___	2. ___	2. ___
3. ___	3. ___	3. ___
4. ___	4. ___	4. ___
5. ___	5. ___	5. ___
6. ___	6. ___	6. ___
7. ___	7. ___	7. ___
8. ___	8. ___	8. ___
9. ___	9. ___	9. ___
10. ___	10. ___	10. ___
11. ___	11. ___	11. ___
12. ___	12. ___	12. ___
13. ___	13. ___	13. ___
14. ___	14. ___	14. ___
15. ___		15. ___
		16. ___
		17. ___
		18. ___
		19. ___
		20. ___

ANSWER KEY - *One Day in the Life of Ivan Denisovich*
Multiple Choice Unit Tests

Answers to Unit Test 1 are in the left column. Answers to Unit Test 2 are in the right column.

I. Matching	II. Multiple Choice	IV. Vocabulary
1. I B	1. C D	1. S C
2. F A	2. B A	2. B O
3. A F	3. B C	3. M T
4. O M	4. A D	4. Q H
5. D P	5. A B	5. O D
6. C J	6. B C	6. T F
7. N L	7. A D	7. A K
8. J C	8. D B	8. G B
9. B Q	9. D C	9. H L
10. L N	10. B A	10. K P
11. P K	11. C A	11. E I
12. Q I	12. C B	12. I A
13. G G	13. D C	13. N R
14. M O	14. A D	14. J Q
15. H E		15. D N
		16. F S
		17. C J
		18. R G
		19. L E
		20. P M

UNIT RESOURCE MATERIALS

BULLETIN BOARD IDEAS - *One Day In The Life of Ivan Denisovich*

1. Save one corner of the board for the best of students' *One Day In The Life of Ivan Denisovich* writing assignments.

2. Take one of the word search puzzles from the extra activities section and with a marker copy it over in a large size on the bulletin board. Write the clue words to find to one side. Invite students prior to and after class to find the words and circle them on the bulletin board.

3. Write several of the most significant quotations from the book onto the board on brightly colored paper.
    > Real jail was when you were kept back from work.
    > And now that he had been given work to do, Shukhov's aches and pains seemed to have gone.
    > When you worked for the knowing, you gave them quality; when you worked for a fool, you simply gave him eyewash.
    > As for the Russians, they've forgotten which hand to cross themselves with.
    > And Shukhov wouldn't take on any old job either. There were others lower than him.
    > The main thing was never to be seen by a camp guard on your own, only in a group.
    > But food gulped down is no food at all; it's wasted; it gives you no feeling of fullness.
    > When he painted the number on your hat with his brush, it was just like a priest anointing your brow.
    > Every nerve in his body was taut, all his longing was concentrated in that cigarette butt-- which was more to him now, it seemed, than freedom itself--but he would never lower himself like that Fetiukov, he would never look at a man's mouth.
    > No one had served his term in this camp.
    > Easy money weighs light in the hand and doesn't give you the feeling you've earned it.
    > Better to growl and submit. If you were stubborn, they broke you.
    > All his memories and worries faded. He had only one idea--to fix the bend in the stovepipe and hang it up to prevent it smoking.
    > . . . But since their day a new decree has been passed, and now the sun stands highest at one.
    > It's not a fact you'll be in all that time. But that I've been in eight full years--now that is a fact.
    > Thank God for a man who does his job and keeps his mouth shut!
    > --nothing must be wasted without good reason.
    > It's no joke to rob five hundred men of over half an hour.
    > Three thousand six hundred and fifty-three days. The three extra days were for leap years.

4. Make a bulletin board listing the vocabulary words for this unit. As you complete sections of the novel and discuss the vocabulary for each section, write the definitions on the bulletin board.

5. Make a bulletin board about Russia: History, Rise and Fall of Communism, or Travel would be good themes to consider.

6. Make a bulletin board about survival--things needed and basic principles to follow.

Denisovich Bulletin Board Ideas Continued

7. Make a bulletin board titled: Facts about Russia. As an introductory activity have each student write up one fact he/she knows about Russia. Use different colored markers. If students know a lot of things or you have a small class, let students write up more than one fact.

8. Make a bulletin board with biographical information about Solzhenitsyn. Make book jackets with summaries of his books inside to post around the biography.

EXTRA ACTIVITIES

One of the difficulties in teaching a novel is that all students don't read at the same speed. One student who likes to read may take the book home and finish it in a day or two. Sometimes a few students finish the in-class assignments early. The problem, then, is finding suitable extra activities for students.

The best thing I've found is to keep a little library in the classroom. For this unit on *One Day In The Life of Ivan Denisovich,* you might check out from the school library other related books and articles about Russian history, communism, current events in Russia, life in prison camps, Russian versus American justice systems, careers in the justice system, construction or other trades, ways to correct injustices, or articles of criticism about *Ivan Denisovich*. Biographical information about the author would be interesting.

Other things you may keep on hand are puzzles. We have made some relating directly to *One Day In The Life of Ivan Denisovich* for you. Feel free to duplicate them.

Some students may like to draw. You might devise a contest or allow some extra-credit grade for students who draw characters or scenes from *One Day In The Life of Ivan Denisovich.* Note, too, that if the students do not want to keep their drawings you may pick up some extra bulletin board materials this way. If you have a contest and you supply the prize (a record album or something like that perhaps), you could, possibly, make the drawing itself a non-refundable entry fee.

The pages which follow contain games, puzzles and worksheets. The keys, when appropriate, immediately follow the puzzle or worksheet. There are two main groups of activities: one group for the unit; that is, generally relating to the *Ivan Denisovich* text, and another group of activities related strictly to the *Ivan Denisovich* vocabulary.

Directions for these games, puzzles and worksheets are self-explanatory. The object here is to provide you with extra materials you may use in any way you choose.

MORE ACTIVITIES - *One Day In The Life of Ivan Denisovich*

1. Pick a chapter or scene with a great deal of dialogue and have the students act it out on a stage. (Perhaps you could assign various scenes to different groups of students so more than one scene could be acted and more students could participate.)

2. Have students design a book cover (front and back and inside flaps) for *One Day In The Life of Ivan Denisovich.*

3. Have students design a bulletin board (ready to be put up; not just sketched) for *One Day In The Life of Ivan Denisovich.*

4. Have students write *One Day in the Life of _____*. (Fill in the name of one of the other characters in the book.) This is a good exercise in point of view and shows students' understanding of the events of the book.

5. Do a mini-unit about the rise and fall of communism in Russia.

6. Show the film version of the book if you can find a copy on video.

7. Discuss some of the quotations from the book. (See bulletin board idea #3.)

8. Take your students to see a state or federal prison.

9. Invite a psychologist in to discuss the psychological effects of work, a work ethic, work as being therapeutic.

10. Discuss ways to cope with being alone, in a new environment, away from the people you love.

WORD SEARCH - *One Day In The Life of Ivan Denisovich*

All words in this list are associated with *One Day In The Life of Ivan Denisovich*. The words are placed backwards, forward, diagonally, up and down. The included words are listed below the word searches.

```
N X M G P L T Y B E Q T C D A P L O T M F Y R S
X P M Y H A T T K R D R O H V U L N Z R O N R G
X Z I C A H R A G S E I S B O V Q D O F O O D S
M A R K O V I C H V V A H S A W E Y E S L W N F
V E N Z N C G U E O K O D P J C O K T R A O E M
Z E S T Q E K I K L M W N K A V C H Y S W E W L
S E R S H O L U Q G S K Y Y O L G O K S R X R F
Q B T P V L Y A S Q U A D K U U Y C T R D R Y T
F R U T E T U T V O T H L N O B A O E Y A W D Q
N X C T E K C F I R C O V H I H R T S T R L H X
R V W F T R I W E L V I T X Y M N H R H S U J F
D A R R L C A L R S A X A D S I S A M K A L I Q
M X T X S M D G G Z U U P L A G T W H B Q N L N
G Z C I C H V W I A C G Q P I Q P G N W V G T S
D S Z G O M G Z L C S O V E R S L E E P I N G X
P B X W X N B R B W P F W V N K T C T K X P Q L
T P H H N Y S T I N E H Z L O S N X M F G F G L
```

ALYOSHA	KASHA	RATIONS	TOBACCO
BREAD	KILGAS	REVEILLE	TREASON
BUTT	MARKOVICH	SENKA	TROWEL
BUYNOVSKY	MESS	SHUKOV	TYRUIN
CIGARETTE	MIND	SNOWSTORMS	USEFUL
DER	MOON	SOCIALIST	VALENKI
EYEWASH	OVERSLEEPING	SOLZHENITSYN	VOLKOVOY
FETYUKOV	PAINTER	SOUL	WOLF
HACKSAW	PARCELS	SQUAD	HAT
PAVLO	TARTAR	HIDE	QUALITY
THOUGHTS			

KEY: WORD SEARCH - *One Day In The Life of Ivan Denisovich*

All words in this list are associated with *One Day In The Life of Ivan Denisovich*. The words are placed backwards, forward, diagonally, up and down. The included words are listed below the word searches.

```
                    P     Y B E   T       A     L O T M
                     A T   K R D R O H   U L N   R O
                 I    A   R A   S E I S B O V   D O F O O        S
          M A R K O V I C H V V A H S A W E Y E S L W N
              E N     N     U E O K O D P   C O   T R A O E
              E S       E K I K L     N   A V C H   S W E W L
          S E     S   O L U     S       Y O L G O K S         R
              B T   V L Y A S Q U A D K U U Y C T R   R     T
                U T E T U T V O     L N O B A O E Y A
                  T E K   F I   C O   H I H R T S T R
              R     F T R I   E L V I T     M N   R H   U
                  A       A L   S A   A   S I   A     A   I
                    T           G G   U U   L A   T             N
                      I       I A   Q P I
                        O       C S O V E R S L E E P I N G
                          N                           T
                          N Y S T I N E H Z L O S
```

ALYOSHA	KASHA	RATIONS	TOBACCO
BREAD	KILGAS	REVEILLE	TREASON
BUTT	MARKOVICH	SENKA	TROWEL
BUYNOVSKY	MESS	SHUKOV	TYRUIN
CIGARETTE	MIND	SNOWSTORMS	USEFUL
DER	MOON	SOCIALIST	VALENKI
EYEWASH	OVERSLEEPING	SOLZHENITSYN	VOLKOVOY
FETYUKOV	PAINTER	SOUL	WOLF
HACKSAW	PARCELS	SQUAD	HAT
PAVLO	TARTAR	HIDE	QUALITY
THOUGHTS			

CROSSWORD - *One Day In The Life of Ivan Denisovich*

CROSSWORD CLUES - *One Day in the Life of Ivan Denisovich*

ACROSS
1. The men wanted to go __ to see their families.
3. Scavenger
6. Ivan hid a ___ blade in his mitten.
11. Oatmeal-type food
12. The Tartar sentenced Ivan to 3 days penalty for ___.
15. Weapon
17. You had to eat with all your --- on the food.
18. Move; begin; start
19. Prison guard
20. It was decreed that it was at its highest point at 1:00
22. Assistant squad leader
24. Mason's tool
25. Here you have time to think about your ----.
26. Old-____ers; those prisoners who had been there for a while
28. End of a cigarette
29. The men were --- from their families; away; separated
31. It was better to --- around a corner than to be seen by a guard alone.
34. Turned to ice
36. Food
38. The Baptist
39. The men --- trowels to do the brick work
40. The experienced prisoners got by by stashing --- things and economizing.
43. Guards needed sharp --- to spot concealed items
45. Gets many parcels
46. Broth
47. Definite article
48. Gang boss
49. Team; group of men
51. Physical labor usually makes one have strong ----
52. Frozen water
53. When you worked for the knowing you gave them ----
54. Author

DOWN
2. --- Hall; place where prisoners eat
4. When you worked for a fool you simply gave him ---.
5. Relatives
6. The --- regulation made it easy for guards to do what they wanted with prisoners.
7. Tsezar Markovich gave Ivan his --- butt instead of giving it to Fetiukov.
8. Had been to Buchenwald
9. 'Volk' means ---.
10. Construction foreman
11. Mason who worked with Ivan
13. Ivan Denisovich
14. Ivan wanted to be a carpet --- after his release.
16. Feeling of hostility
17. The people of Ivan's village say God crumbles the old --- to make stars.
21. Captain
23. Winter shoes
27. That one (pronoun)
28. Ivan hid his to eat later so it wouldn't be stolen.
30. Ivan volunteered to stand in line at the --- office for Tsezar.
32. The --- of a prisoner--they're not free either.
33. They were both a blessing and a curse to prisoners.
35. --- Way of Life Settlement
37. Sick
41. Ivan was incarcerated as a punishment for high --
42. Ivan went to Lett's room after dinner to buy it
44. Sneaky
50. Present plural of 'to be'

CROSSWORD ANSWER KEY - *One Day In The Life of Ivan Denisovich*

MATCHING QUIZ/WORKSHEET 1 - *One Day In The Life of Ivan Denisovich*

___ 1. SOLZHENITSYN   A. In charge of discipline

___ 2. PAVLO   B. Had been to Buchenwald

___ 3. TROWEL   C. Team; group of men

___ 4. USEFUL   D. Author

___ 5. BREAD   E. --- Hall; place where prisoners eat

___ 6. SQUAD   F. Mason's tool

___ 7. SENKA   G. Ivan volunteered to stand in line at the --- office for Tsezar.

___ 8. RATIONS   H. Ivan Denisovich

___ 9. SOUL   I. Ivan wanted to be a carpet --- after his release.

___ 10. FETYUKOV   J. The people of Ivan's village say God crumbles the old --- to make stars.

___ 11. EYEWASH   K. --- Way of Life Settlement

___ 12. PARCELS   L. Ivan went to Lett's room after dinner to buy it.

___ 13. MESS   M. Oatmeal-type food

___ 14. SOCIALIST   N. The experienced prisoners got by by stashing --- things and economizing.

___ 15. SHUKHOV   O. When you worked for a fool you simply gave him ---.

___ 16. PAINTER   P. Food

___ 17. KASHA   Q. Scavenger

___ 18. VOLKOVOY   R. Ivan hid his to eat later so it wouldn't be stolen.

___ 19. MOON   S. Assistant squad leader

___ 20. TOBACCO   T. Here you have time to think about your ----.

KEY: MATCHING QUIZ/WORKSHEET 1 - *One Day In The Life of Ivan Denisovich*

<u>D</u> 1. SOLZHENITSYN   A. In charge of discipline

<u>S</u> 2. PAVLO   B. Had been to Buchenwald

<u>F</u> 3. TROWEL   C. Team; group of men

<u>N</u> 4. USEFUL   D. Author

<u>R</u> 5. BREAD   E. --- Hall; place where prisoners eat

<u>C</u> 6. SQUAD   F. Mason's tool

<u>B</u> 7. SENKA   G. Ivan volunteered to stand in line at the --- office for Tsezar.

<u>P</u> 8. RATIONS   H. Ivan Denisovich

<u>T</u> 9. SOUL   I. Ivan wanted to be a carpet --- after his release.

<u>Q</u> 10. FETYUKOV   J. The people of Ivan's village say God crumbles the old --- to make stars.

<u>O</u> 11. EYEWASH   K. --- Way of Life Settlement

<u>G</u> 12. PARCELS   L. Ivan went to Lett's room after dinner to buy it.

<u>E</u> 13. MESS   M. Oatmeal-type food

<u>K</u> 14. SOCIALIST   N. The experienced prisoners got by by stashing --- things and economizing.

<u>H</u> 15. SHUKHOV   O. When you worked for a fool you simply gave him ---.

<u>I</u> 16. PAINTER   P. Food

<u>M</u> 17. KASHA   Q. Scavenger

<u>A</u> 18. VOLKOVOY   R. Ivan hid his to eat later so it wouldn't be stolen.

<u>J</u> 19. MOON   S. Assistant squad leader

<u>L</u> 20. TOBACCO   T. Here you have time to think about your ----.

MATCHING QUIZ/WORKSHEET 2 - *One Day In The Life of Ivan Denisovich*

___ 1. RATIONS	A. Here you have time to think about your ----.

___ 2. REVEILLE	B. Ivan Denisovich

___ 3. OVERSLEEPING	C. Tsezar Markovich gave Ivan his --- butt instead of giving it to Fetiukov.

___ 4. TARTAR	D. Ivan hid his to eat later so it wouldn't be stolen.

___ 5. VOLKOVOY	E. Call to get up

___ 6. TROWEL	F. The --- regulation made it easy for guards to do what they wanted with prisoners.

___ 7. EYEWASH	G. The Tartar sentenced Ivan to 3 days penalty for ---.

___ 8. TIURIN	H. Ivan hid a --- blade in his mitten.

___ 9. SOUL	I. Team; group of men

___ 10. PAINTER	J. Food

___ 11. SQUAD	K. Author

___ 12. SNOWSTORMS	L. They were both a blessing and a curse to prisoners.

___ 13. BREAD	M. Prison guard

___ 14. HACKSAW	N. Gang boss

___ 15. SHUKHOV	O. --- Way of Life Settlement

___ 16. SOLZHENITSYN	P. Ivan wanted to be a carpet --- after his release.

___ 17. CIGARETTE	Q. When you worked for a fool you simply gave him ---.

___ 18. SOCIALIST	R. In charge of discipline

___ 19. MOON	S. Mason's tool

___ 20. HAT	T. God crumbles the old --- to make stars.

KEY: MATCHING QUIZ/WORKSHEET 2 - *One Day In The Life of Ivan Denisovich*

_J_ 1. RATIONS	A. Here you have time to think about your ----.
_E_ 2. REVEILLE	B. Ivan Denisovich
_G_ 3. OVERSLEEPING	C. Tsezar Markovich gave Ivan his --- butt instead of giving it to Fetiukov.
_M_ 4. TARTAR	D. Ivan hid his to eat later so it wouldn't be stolen.
_R_ 5. VOLKOVOY	E. Call to get up
_S_ 6. TROWEL	F. The --- regulation made it easy for guards to do what they wanted with prisoners.
_Q_ 7. EYEWASH	G. The Tartar sentenced Ivan to 3 days penalty for ---.
_N_ 8. TIURIN	H. Ivan hid a --- blade in his mitten.
_A_ 9. SOUL	I. Team; group of men
_P_ 10. PAINTER	J. Food
_I_ 11. SQUAD	K. Author
_L_ 12. SNOWSTORMS	L. They were both a blessing and a curse to prisoners.
_D_ 13. BREAD	M. Prison guard
_H_ 14. HACKSAW	N. Gang boss
_B_ 15. SHUKHOV	O. --- Way of Life Settlement
_K_ 16. SOLZHENITSYN	P. Ivan wanted to be a carpet --- after his release.
_C_ 17. CIGARETTE	Q. When you worked for a fool you simply gave him ---.
_O_ 18. SOCIALIST	R. In charge of discipline
_T_ 19. MOON	S. Mason's tool
_F_ 20. HAT	T. God crumbles the old --- to make stars.

JUGGLE LETTER REVIEW GAME CLUE SHEET
One Day In The Life of Ivan Denisovich

SCRAMBLED	WORD	CLUE
SHKAA	KASHA	Oatmeal-type food
FLWO	WOLF	'Volk' means _____
ETCGTIREA	CIGARETTE	Tsezar Markovich gave Ivan his _____ butt instead of giving it to Fetiukov
VLIREEEL	REVEILLE	Call to get up
NOMRTSWSSO	SNOWSTORMS	They were both a blessing and a curse to prisoners.
EDIH	HIDE	It was better to _____ around a corner than to be seen by a guard alone
SMSE	MESS	_____ Hall; place where prisoners eat
UTBT	BUTT	End of a cigarette
LUUSFE	USEFUL	The experienced prisoners got by by stashing _____ things and economizing
STIRNOA	RATIONS	Food
ELPSRCA	PARCELS	Ivan volunteered to stand in line at the _____ office for Tsezar
NTAROSE	TREASON	Ivan was incarcerated as a punishment for high _____.
KVHUSOH	SHUKHOV	Ivan Denisovich
ERD	DER	Construction Foreman
QUADS	SQUAD	Team; group of men
LOAPV	PAVLO	Assistant squad leader
OBCCOTA	TOBACCO	Ivan went to Lett's room after dinner to buy it
EIKNLAV	VALENKI	Winter shoes
YSALHAO	ALYOSHA	The Baptist
YOOVLVKO	VOLKOVOY	In charge of discipline
UTGSHTOH	THOUGHTS	The _____ of a prisoner--they're not free either
EIUVFOKT	FETIUKOV	Scavenger
ASHEYEW	EYEWASH	When you worked for a fool you simply gave him _____.
NMOO	MOON	The people of Ivan's village say God crumbles the old _____ to make stars
ATH	HAT	The _____ regulation made it easy for guards to do what they wanted with prisoners
LUOS	SOUL	Here you have time to think about your _____.
EINOVRLEGPES	OVERSLEEPING	The Tartar sentenced Ivan to 3 days penalty for _____.
OHCRKAMIV	MARKOVICH	Gets many parcels

VOCABULARY RESOURCE MATERIALS

VOCABULARY WORD SEARCH - *One Day In The Life of Ivan Denisovich*

All words in this list are associated with *One Day In The Life of Ivan Denisovich* with an emphasis on the vocabulary words chosen for study in the text. The words are placed backwards, forward, diagonally, up and down. The included words are listed below.

```
S F D V J Y F E T V V Y K C Q Y E V X T W X R R
L T R C B N T T G W I Y Y V U K A S P F U F L G
A C Q U I R I N G D I C N A R R E V U E N A M Y
Z L F D F N I N A M U N I O R B T R S R E Z T J
I F L G M N T Y E C A R G O K X Y A N Z C C P H
L M G O N O J E L R S D G E U C J M I P X F G N
C A P U C S C F R G T A V E Y S E T F L R V O P
S O C E C A R K C M N P H O B X U B W Q E I X V
Z Z N I R O T B E C I I B K C N F O T Q T D Q K
R B R T T T N I E R F T R L M A P Z I A W G N R
C S P S I C U S N T Y R T E Z Y T S X C C F Z B
M O D X H N A R U G N W P E H R C E Q M I N R Q
X K N D T P G R B L W L B R N T V C D S D L J L
P S X C T G Y E P A T R H D Z T I B B L D B A D
S N R S E T C T N M B I G P N N Z W V J W Y R M
Z M Y W F A N Z G C I L N K W Y P X R C C K G Y
K X H V B C L S Z R Y D E G Q G F R G F Q F H G
```

ACQUIRING	CONTINGENCY	INTERMITTENT	TWINGE
ADVOCATED	CUNNING	MALICIOUS	VEXATION
ALLOCATING	CURTAILED	MANEUVER	VICIOUS
ARROGANCE	DIN	MOCKERY	WITHERINGLY
BECKON	FURY	RANCID	ZEAL
BEGRUDGE	IMPERTURBABLE	RUSE	CONCEAL
IMPRACTICAL	SCANTY	CONSULTING	INERT
TAUT			

KEY: VOCABULARY WORD SEARCH - *One Day In The Life of Ivan Denisovich*

All words in this list are associated with *One Day In The Life of Ivan Denisovich* with an emphasis on the vocabulary words chosen for study in the text. The words are placed backwards, forward, diagonally, up and down. The included words are listed below.

```
                    Y    E T V         C       E        T
                    N T   G W I        U     A S      F U     L
         A C Q U I R I N G D I C N A R R E V U E N A M
           L   D   N I N A   U N I O R   T R   R E     T
         I   L   M N T Y E C A R G O K   Y A   Z
         L M   O N O   E L R S D G E U C     I             N
         C A P U C   C   R G T A V E   S E     L         O
           O C E C A   K   M N     O B   U B     E I
             N I R O T   E C I I     C       O     T D
               T T T N I E R   T R       A     I A
         C         I C U S N   Y   T E     T   X C
             O       N A R U G       E H     E     I
               N       G R B L         N T V   D     L
                   C     E P A T         T I         A
                     E     N M B I           W           M
                       A     C I L N
                         L     Y E G
```

ACQUIRING   CONTINGENCY   INTERMITTENT   TWINGE
ADVOCATED   CUNNING   MALICIOUS   VEXATION
ALLOCATING   CURTAILED   MANEUVER   VICIOUS
ARROGANCE   DIN   MOCKERY   WITHERINGLY
BECKON   FURY   RANCID   ZEAL
BEGRUDGE   INERT   RUSE   CONCEAL
IMPRACTICAL   SCANTY   CONSULTING   TAUT
IMPERTURBABLE

VOCABULARY CROSSWORD - One Day In The Life of Ivan Denisovich

VOCABULARY CROSSWORD CLUES - *One Day in the Life of Ivan Denisovich*

ACROSS
1. Rage; anger
4. Seeking advice or information from someone
7. Assistant squad leader
11. A controlled change in movement, direction or position
13. To make a summoning gesture
15. End of a cigarette
16. Sight organ
18. Eat dinner
20. Construction foreman
22. The art of subtlety and deceptiveness
23. Overbearing pride
25. Belonging to us
26. Surround
27. 'Volk' means ---.
28. Affirmative answer
32. A sudden, sharp emotional or physical pain
35. Supported the cause or idea of something
38. --- Way of Life Settlement
39. --- Hall; place where prisoners eat
41. ___-fink; an informer
42. Weapon
43. The experienced prisoners got by by stashing --- things and economizing.
45. Definite article
47. Gaining possession of
48. Stopping and starting at intervals

DOWN
2. A crafty strategy; a diversion
3. The --- regulation made it easy for guards to do what they wanted with prisoners
4. A possibility that must be prepared for
5. Barely sufficient; a small amount
6. Tight; in shape; tense
8. Exclusive right or privilege to choose
9. Ivan hid his to eat later so it wouldn't be stolen
10. Ridiculing; jeering at; making fun of
12. Spoiled; gone bad
13. Envy the possession or enjoyment of
14. Cut short
17. Savage; faulty; foul
18. A jumble of loud, discordant sounds
19. Unable to move or act
21. The Baptist
24. Distributing according to a plan
29. It was better to --- around a corner than to be seen by a guard alone.
30. Oatmeal-type food
31. Zest; energy
33. Prison guard
34. Mason who worked with Ivan
36. Annoyance
37. Hide
39. The Moldavian was ___ at the count
40. Here you have time to think about your ----.
44. The people of Ivan's village say God crumbles the old --- to make stars.
46. You had to eat with all your --- on the food

VOCABULARY CROSSWORD ANSWER KEY - *One Day In The Life of Ivan Denisovich*

VOCABULARY WORKSHEET 1 - *One Day In The Life of Ivan Denisovich*

___ 1. ALLOCATING   A. A controlled change in movement, direction or position

___ 2. IMPRACTICAL   B. Not practical in nature; can't see or implement useful ideas

___ 3. INERT   C. Cut short

___ 4. ADVOCATED   D. Unshakably calm and collected

___ 5. CONTINGENCY   E. Overbearing pride

___ 6. TWINGE   F. Zest; energy

___ 7. MANEUVER   G. Tight; in shape; tense

___ 8. TAUT   H. Spoiled; gone bad

___ 9. RANCID   I. The art of subtlety and deceptiveness

___ 10. INTERMITTENT   J. Ridiculing; jeering at; making fun of

___ 11. ARROGANCE   K. Stopping and starting at intervals

___ 12. CUNNING   L. To make a summoning gesture

___ 13. FURY   M. Unable to move or act

___ 14. MOCKERY   N. Rage; anger

___ 15. IMPERTURBABLE   O. A possibility that must be prepared for

___ 16. ZEAL   P. Gaining possession of

___ 17. CURTAILED   Q. Supported the cause or idea of something

___ 18. BEGRUDGE   R. Envy the possession or enjoyment of

___ 19. BECKON   S. Distributing according to a plan

___ 20. ACQUIRING   T. A sudden, sharp emotional or physical pain

KEY: VOCABULARY WORKSHEET 1 - *One Day In The Life of Ivan Denisovich*

_S_	1. ALLOCATING	A. A controlled change in movement, direction or position
_B_	2. IMPRACTICAL	B. Not practical in nature; can't see or implement useful ideas
_M_	3. INERT	C. Cut short
_Q_	4. ADVOCATED	D. Unshakably calm and collected
_O_	5. CONTINGENCY	E. Overbearing pride
_T_	6. TWINGE	F. Zest; energy
_A_	7. MANEUVER	G. Tight; in shape; tense
_G_	8. TAUT	H. Spoiled; gone bad
_H_	9. RANCID	I. The art of subtlety and deceptiveness
_K_	10. INTERMITTENT	J. Ridiculing; jeering at; making fun of
_E_	11. ARROGANCE	K. Stopping and starting at intervals
_I_	12. CUNNING	L. To make a summoning gesture
_N_	13. FURY	M. Unable to move or act
_J_	14. MOCKERY	N. Rage; anger
_D_	15. IMPERTURBABLE	O. A possibility that must be prepared for
_F_	16. ZEAL	P. Gaining possession of
_C_	17. CURTAILED	Q. Supported the cause or idea of something
_R_	18. BEGRUDGE	R. Envy the possession or enjoyment of
_L_	19. BECKON	S. Distributing according to a plan
_P_	20. ACQUIRING	T. A sudden, sharp emotional or physical pain

VOCABULARY WORKSHEET 2 - *One Day In The Life of Ivan Denisovich*

___ 1. Gaining possession of
    a. Vicious   b. Cunning   c. Begrudge   d. Acquiring

___ 2. Unable to move or act
    a. Inert   b. Witheringly   c. Taut   d. Scanty

___ 3. A crafty strategy; a diversion
    a. Inert   b. Vexation   c. Ruse   d. Zeal

___ 4. The art of subtlety and deceptiveness
    a. Allocating   b. Impractical   c. Cunning   d. Conceal

___ 5. Unshakably calm and collected
    a. Curtailed   b. Imperturbable   c. Inert   d. Acquiring

___ 6. Stopping and starting at intervals
    a. Intermittent   b. Contingency   c. Conceal   d. Twinge

___ 7. Distributing according to a plan
    a. Consulting   b. Allocating   c. Din   d. Cunning

___ 8. A jumble of loud, discordant sounds
    a. Malicious   b. Twinge   c. Din   d. Witheringly

___ 9. Rage; anger
    a. Beckon   b. Fury   c. Contingency   d. Begrudge

___ 10. Cut short
    a. Zeal   b. Curtailed   c. Vicious   d. Scanty

___ 11. Barely sufficient; a small amount
    a. Scanty   b. Arrogance   c. Contingency   d. Witheringly

___ 12. Seeking advice or information from someone
    a. Conceal   b. Acquiring   c. Consulting   d. Prerogative

___ 13. To make a summoning gesture
    a. Twinge   b. Conceal   c. Beckon   d. Impractical

___ 14. Ridiculing; jeering at; making fun of
    a. Mockery   b. Begrudge   c. Cunning   d. Conceal

___ 15. Exclusive right or privilege to choose
    a. Consulting   b. Ruse   c. Curtailed   d. Prerogative

___ 16. Showing a desire to see others suffer
    a. Malicious   b. Ruse   c. Witheringly   d. Scanty

___ 17. A sudden, sharp emotional or physical pain
    a. Advocated   b. Twinge   c. Prerogative   d. Impractical

___ 18. Spoiled; gone bad
    a. Rancid   b. Conceal   c. Consulting   d. Impractical

___ 19. A controlled change in movement, direction or position
    a. Maneuver   b. Inert   c. Vicious   d. Twinge

___ 20. Not practical in nature; can't see or implement useful ideas
    a. Impractical   b. Scanty   c. Cunning   d. Fury

KEY: VOCABULARY WORKSHEET 2 - *One Day In The Life of Ivan Denisovich*

__D__ 1. Gaining possession of
    a. Vicious   b. Cunning   c. Begrudge   d. Acquiring

__A__ 2. Unable to move or act
    a. Inert   b. Witheringly   c. Taut   d. Scanty

__C__ 3. A crafty strategy; a diversion
    a. Inert   b. Vexation   c. Ruse   d. Zeal

__C__ 4. The art of subtlety and deceptiveness
    a. Allocating   b. Impractical   c. Cunning   d. Conceal

__B__ 5. Unshakably calm and collected
    a. Curtailed   b. Imperturbable   c. Inert   d. Acquiring

__A__ 6. Stopping and starting at intervals
    a. Intermittent   b. Contingency   c. Conceal   d. Twinge

__B__ 7. Distributing according to a plan
    a. Consulting   b. Allocating   c. Din   d. Cunning

__C__ 8. A jumble of loud, discordant sounds
    a. Malicious   b. Twinge   c. Din   d. Witheringly

__B__ 9. Rage; anger
    a. Beckon   b. Fury   c. Contingency   d. Begrudge

__B__ 10. Cut short
    a. Zeal   b. Curtailed   c. Vicious   d. Scanty

__A__ 11. Barely sufficient; a small amount
    a. Scanty   b. Arrogance   c. Contingency   d. Witheringly

__C__ 12. Seeking advice or information from someone
    a. Conceal   b. Acquiring   c. Consulting   d. Prerogative

__C__ 13. To make a summoning gesture
    a. Twinge   b. Conceal   c. Beckon   d. Impractical

__A__ 14. Ridiculing; jeering at; making fun of
    a. Mockery   b. Begrudge   c. Cunning   d. Conceal

__D__ 15. Exclusive right or privilege to choose
    a. Consulting   b. Ruse   c. Curtailed   d. Prerogative

__A__ 16. Showing a desire to see others suffer
    a. Malicious   b. Ruse   c. Witheringly   d. Scanty

__B__ 17. A sudden, sharp emotional or physical pain
    a. Advocated   b. Twinge   c. Prerogative   d. Impractical

__A__ 18. Spoiled; gone bad
    a. Rancid   b. Conceal   c. Consulting   d. Impractical

__A__ 19. A controlled change in movement, direction or position
    a. Maneuver   b. Inert   c. Vicious   d. Twinge

__A__ 20. Not practical in nature; can't see or implement useful ideas
    a. Impractical   b. Scanty   c. Cunning   d. Fury

VOCABULARY REVIEW GAME CLUES - *One Day In The Life of Ivan Denisovich*

SCRAMBLED	WORD	CLUE
ICULSMIOA	MALICIOUS	Showing a desire to see others suffer
EOBNCK	BECKON	To make a summoning gesture
UCISVOI	VICIOUS	Savage; faulty; foul
ARVEMUNE	MANEUVER	A controlled change in movement, direction or position
RACEAOGRN	ARROGANCE	Overbearing pride
UTTA	TAUT	Tight; in shape; tense
NGUCNNI	CUNNING	The art of subtlety and deceptiveness
ERITN	INERT	Unable to move or act
IEGEPRVROTA	PREROGATIVE	Exclusive right or privilege to choose
GUREEGDB	BEGRUDGE	Envy the possession or enjoyment of
IND	DIN	A jumble of loud, discordance sounds
ERYOKMC	MOCKERY	Ridiculing; jeering at; making fun of
RCALTDEIU	CURTAILED	Cut short
USER	RUSE	A crafty strategy; a diversion
CNLOACE	CONCEAL	Hide
NUILNTCOGS	CONSULTING	Seeking advice or information from someone
AEDVDCAOT	ADVOCATED	Supported the cause or idea of something
AONGATLLCI	ALLOCATING	Distributing according to a plan
ACIMCIATLPR	IMPRACTICAL	Not practical in nature; can't see or implement useful ideas
YGIIWLRHTEN	WITHERINGLY	Devastatingly
IVAONXTE	VEXATION	Annoyance
ITTMNNRIETTE	INTERMITTENT	Stopping and starting at intervals
YSCTNA	SCANTY	Barely sufficient; a small amount
NQIRIGCUA	ACQUIRING	Gaining possession of
EALZ	ZEAL	Zest; energy
NCIRDA	RANCID	Spoiled; gone bad
UFYR	FURY	Rage; anger
ETMBPIEUARLBR	IMPERTURBABLE	Unshakably calm and collected

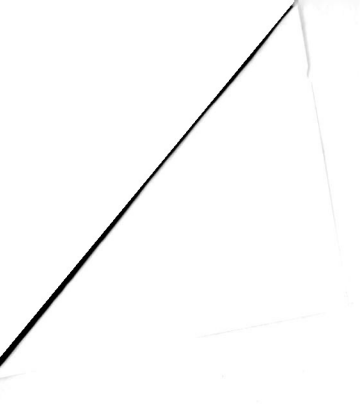

www.ingramcontent.com/pod-product-compliance
Lightning Source LLC
Chambersburg PA
CBHW051417070526
44584CB00023B/3467